THE CONQUEST OF MISERY

By

F. KIPP NOYES

ISBN: 0-75962-526-3

This book is printed on acid free paper.

1stBooks - rev. 7/03/01

*There is no such thing as a moral
or immoral book. Books are well
written or badly written. That is all.*
                    —Oscar Wilde

TABLE OF CONTENTS

<u>PREFACE</u>

This is not supposed to be a sales pitch. Even though it may not sound like it, this is an encouragement for you to read this book.

I must confess that I've known F. Kipp Noyes for some time, and I understand and accept most of his ideas about the origins of misery. Personalities aside, the information he has compiled here is some of the most provocative stuff I've run across in my career.

You should know that Mr. Noyes asked me to write this preface. More exactly, he invited me to do it if I wanted. I did want to and I'm very proud to sign my statement.

I consider myself to be an expert in the field of psychiatry. I've been in the business of dealing with people's emotional problems for over fifteen years. In that time I think I can truthfully say that I've seen it all. Of course, in my next hundred years of practice I'll probably see a lot more. Based on my knowledge of how my clients got to the point where they needed my help, there is no doubt in my mind that the causes of misery Mr. Noyes has set out here, although there are only ten of them, are real, and they do cause a lot of needless suffering. As to the cures, I'm not such an expert regarding some of them. From what I know personally about the others, they are the most effective I've discovered. By interpolation, since the cures are responsive to the causes, I feel confident in assuming that all the cures are effective.

Although the purpose of the preface is not to talk you into reading a book, but give some background on how and why it was created, I think my point is still clear! I hope you do read it!

Mr. Noyes makes no bones about where the ideas he has gathered together come from. Some of them are his ideas. Others have filtered into memory and become a part of his thinking. It doesn't make much difference that all the ideas aren't original. What does matter is that they work. And they do...well!

I'm proud to write the Preface for "The Conquest of Misery," and I heartily encourage you to read it all the way through. If you don't finish the book, at least think about what you have read. I'm sure you will be well rewarded in understanding and compassion for your efforts.

—Sylvia Masters, M. D.

Editors Note: Dr. Masters is the author of several self-help books for laymen. Among her best known are: *You Can Overcome Your Fears* and *All About Love*.

When she is not writing, Dr. Masters is in private psychiatric practice in San Francisco, California.

<u>INTRODUCTION</u>

Resolve to be thyself and know that he who finds himself loses his misery.
—Matthew Arnold

Probably before the dawn of man's recorded history upon this planet, philosophies were introduced, methods offered and theories propounded for the elimination of misery from the human race. Certainly since man started keeping records new ways of dealing with the world have been arising, but they have never completely achieved their goal.

Certainly this is another philosophy, another way of looking at the inner workings of man. It is different in that it takes pieces of information that have proven true and workable, combined them with other ideas, theories, some of them unique, to come up with a broader picture of man's misery, its causes and consequent cures. If some of the ideas are not new, the overall methods of conquering misery are still valuable.

In order to more fully understand and more deeply appreciate the human condition, what causes misery and how it can be alleviated, it is first necessary to have a basic understanding of how its various parts are interrelated.

If you look at man as a complex organism with various parts that somehow work together in unison, it becomes easier to visualize the interrelationships that exist. Since man is not a simple creature, it is necessary to understand how his segments function relative to the *whole* of his being.

In esoteric philosophy, the three levels of man's functioning are usually called "planes of existence." They basically designate different levels and complexity of operation. To make the interrelationship of these three parts of man's nature more graphic, it is easier to see them as spheres of being.

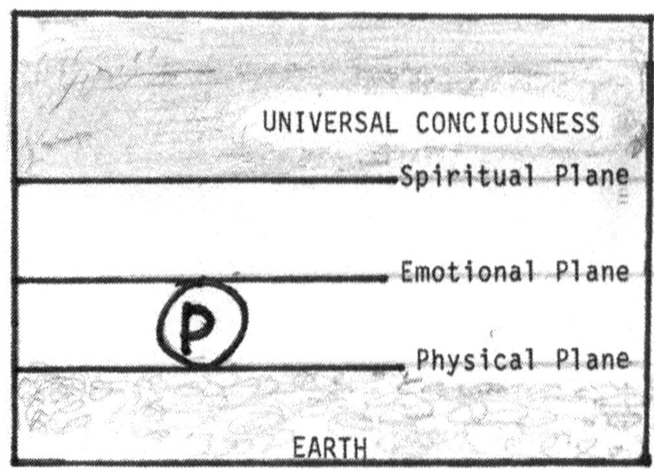

ILLUSTRATION 1

The sphere of man's existence with which we're most familiar is the physical. This represents the basic gross structure of man: his body. Physical functioning is simply how the body works, what it does and why.

To see how the three spheres are different, yet the same, think of the physical sphere as being that part of man which is closest to the earth, the most basic part of a human being. If you visualize the physical sphere of man as touching the ground, (think of his feet touching the earth), the other two spheres of being seem more natural configurations, being like the upper portions of a human figure.

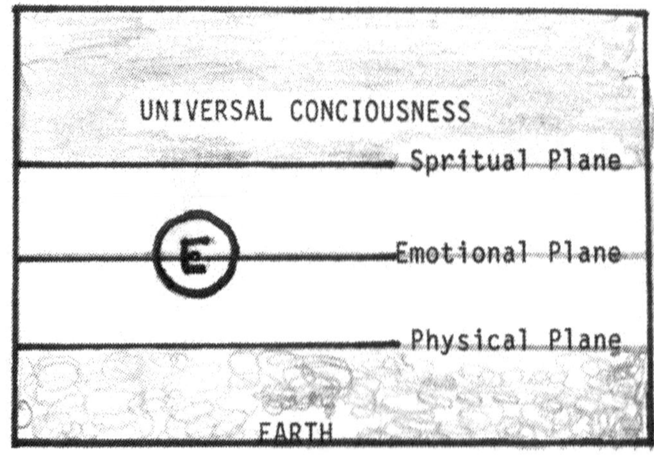

ILLUSTRATION 2

The next sphere of man's being is the emotional. On a graphic level, if you think of the emotional sphere as being above the physical, it is easier to see the higher and more complicated functioning involved. Where man's feet are firmly planted on the ground, his emotions are created on an upper level, in his head.

Man has set himself above other creatures on this planet, not because of biological superiority, but by his ability to reason through problems and to come to conclusions not necessarily based on his own experience. Man is capable of developing workable solutions to novel situations through this unique ability.

Man's brain directs his movements and the actions of his physical body. When the brain senses the need for an action, it conveys this information to the muscles or other systems of the body to perform as required. The brain is the physical organ that directs the other organs. This functioning is on a higher level than the physical, but it is still based primarily in the lower sphere of being.

The emotions are a product of the brain, but are not controlled exclusively by it. They have another influence swaying them. If an occasion occurs for us to cry, the emotions react to the stimulus, compute, correlate information and *direct the brain* to start the tear ducts overflowing, the heart rate to change, and breathing to speed up. The brain directs the other organs. The emotions create a different, illogical reaction also. We *feel sadness*. That feeling is not physical, but comes from the higher sphere of being, the emotional.

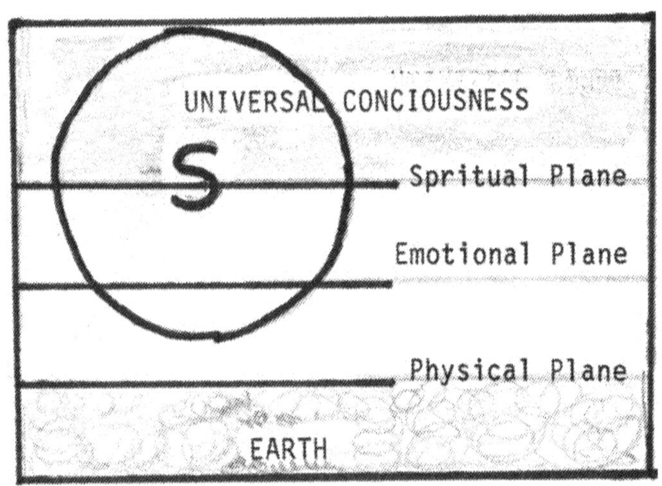

ILLUSTRATION 3

The third sphere of man's being which influences the reactions of his physical and emotional spheres is the spiritual. This is the part of man that sits above the other two. It receives information from the nonphysical, psychic world and transmits data down to the emotional sphere that in turn directs the physical nature.

Think of the spiritual sphere as an extension of man. Visualize man and his place on this planet. The physical sphere of his being, his baser nature, is represented by his feet firmly planted on the earth, the material plane of existence. The emotional sphere, a higher level of functioning, like his head, is near the earth, but not connected too closely to it. The spiritual sphere is above both of these, contacting Universal Consciousness, the "other world" where nonphysical information can be contacted. If you can visualize a place above the emotional sphere that reaches from man's second highest nature, his head, up toward outer space, past that, to the infinite universe, spiritual functioning becomes less difficult to comprehend. It is not connected to man's physical or emotional spheres, yet the spiritual is all around him, like the spaces in which he walks.

Spiritual functioning in the nonphysical world isn't so mysterious and unknowable. It is simply an extension of man's nature which surpasses the material plane and extends into Universal Consciousness where all information, knowledge and wisdom, past, present and future is stored.

Universal Consciousness, called by many other names, can be thought of as a huge department store wherein the spiritual sphere can shop around and find useful information, rather like man can shop for his own food in a grocery store. In this higher world, the spiritual sphere of being performs its work.

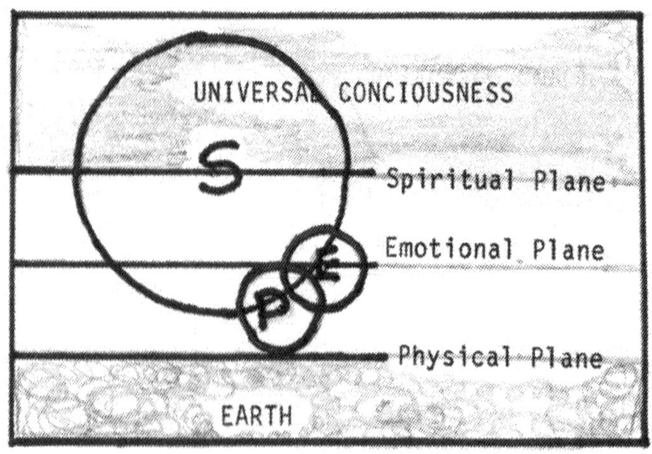

<u>ILLUSTRATION 4</u>

As you can see by visualizing the three levels of existence as spheres occupying different parts of space, their functioning is graphically presented. The spiritual sphere, the highest level of man's being, makes partial contact with both the emotional and physical spheres. The emotional sphere makes contact with the physical and spiritual spheres and the physical sphere makes contact with the higher two. There is even a place where all three contribute their various functioning to one reaction. It is at these intersections of influence, where strong interrelationships are present, that the most severe misery can be created.

The how and why of the creation of misery is dealt with in detail in this book. Part I describes the most basic causes of misery, how the various spheres work upon and with each other and why misery is sometimes the result. Part II examines some possible cures for these causes of misery and some solutions to seemingly complex problems.

In part III a method for implementing the cures is introduced. *The Church of Psychic Sanctuary* is an organization with the sole purpose of determining causes of and finding cures to misery. Its evolution, from idea to concept to reality, is set out.

In all parts of this book, even to the Bibliography and other Appendices, one goal is always in sight: the elimination and eradication of unhappiness and sorrow from this planet. The whole purpose of this book and the Church is simple:

<u>THE CONQUEST OF MISERY</u>.

PART 1:
THE CAUSES OF MISERY

Every man is the builder of a
temple called his body.
　　　　—Henry David Thoreau

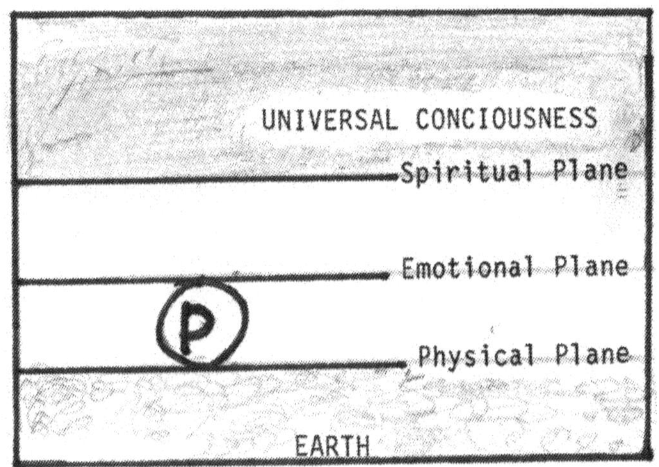

ILLUSTRATION 5

PHYSICAL CAUSES

Since the physical sphere of man's being is nearest the earth, and consequently nearest his material world, it is a logical place to start our analysis of the causes of misery.

Physical problems affect the other spheres of being at their nearest proximity where their influences are shared. Through physical ills, negative energy is transmitted to either or both of the other two spheres, thereby causing misery.

CONSTRICTION OF BODY FREEDOM

One of the most obvious and simple causes of misery in the physical sphere is the artificial hampering of man's body movement. Primarily, clothing brings about this constraint of physical freedom.

Clothing has a definite purpose in man's physical existence upon this planet: it effectively protects him from the elements. That is the only real necessity for clothing. However, clothing is used for a variety of other purposes today, none of which is natural.

We must digress at this point. In analyzing the causes of and cures to misery, as in any discussion of man and his reactions to his environment, certain words keep coming up which must be clearly defined. They are terms that describe man's relationships, modify them and bring them into the realm of practical experience rather than confining them to theory. All of the important words can be found in the Glossary in the back of this book, but here are two of them that crop up most often.

3

The first is the word "natural". When our interrelationships with our environment, our states of being and our perceptions are innate and instinctual, the way we "feel" rather than the way we think, they are *natural* reactions. When our reactions become affected by social conditioning or by premeditation for other reasons, they can become *unnatural*.

The second is the word "healthy". Anything that aids our well being, makes us feel better, increases our effectiveness as successful members of the species— it is *healthy* because it is life enhancing. Destructive behavior, reactions that make us unsuccessful in our endeavors, things that threaten our well being are *unhealthy.*

By looking at our reactions and interrelationships with these words in mind, the reasons we deal with our environment the way we do becomes clear. Almost every action we take can be seen as being natural or unnatural, healthy or unhealthy, positive or negative, happy or miserable.

Back to the subject. The most blatantly unnatural use of clothing occurs in a social convention. With an ever-increasing population occupying less and less available space on this planet, society believes that man's unrestrained nakedness would lead to an abundance of social problems. Since man is basically an erotic creature, he believes the nakedness of others near him might lead to "immoral" sexual behavior; behavior society sees as disruptive, destructive and anti-social. By wearing clothing man hides his nakedness, his image as an erotic provocateur and thereby, in society's view, eases possible problems of moral decadence.

This, of course, is an over simplification. There are other reasons for the social convention. However, as a deterrent to erotic behavior, the convention probably predates man's recorded history on this planet.

In past cultures nakedness has not always been perceived as "sinful" or equated with immoral behavior. In fact, there have been times in man's history when nakedness was considered a simple part of life, an expression of man's natural condition. Although they, too, had the social convention of clothing, nakedness still had a definite respected place in the natural order of things.

Though there are fewer and fewer of them that remain unchanged, in primitive societies today nakedness is considered to be a virtue. A natural expression is encouraged. These primitive societies have clothing, but its function is more for displaying and adorning the body, than for hiding its nakedness. They do not have the same social convention we do, yet they have little problem with immoral, disruptive behavior.

One purpose of clothing, which modifies the social convention and makes imagination into acceptable social behavior, is for it to serve as a healthy extension of man's personality. By changing our manner of dress, we can express our changing emotional nature. No matter if colors are quiet or loud, what style, whether conservative or flamboyant, fit, whether it is loose and relaxed or tight and full of vital animal energy, can express how we feel about ourselves. Healthy or not, the wearing of clothing is unnatural for any reason other than protecting the body against the elements.

Social conditioning, the learning of the convention, begins early in our life and stays with us forever. Through this conditioning of our brain, our natural reaction to stimuli is altered.

No matter how soft, fabric grates upon the skin. It causes constriction of muscle movement and irritates the sensitive nerve endings that perceive the cloth as a foreign substance. These irritations to the body send a constant stream of distress signals to the brain, begging for some remedial action.

After having been conditioned by social convention and unconsciously altering our natural condition, our brain becomes numb to our body's artificial bondage. Since they are constantly barraging the brain with their complaints, the warning signs of irritation slowly become like background noise to the mind.

The natural reaction to the negative stimulus caused by the fabric would be to get rid of the irritation, to take off the clothes. Since society dictates that we cannot do that under many conditions, the mind is unable to command the body's appropriate reaction. It therefore bypasses these distress signals so that it won't have to make contradictory decisions. The brain's natural reaction to take off the clothes must be sublimated in favor of the social convention to keep them on.

When the brain is forced not to react *naturally*, when it is denied permission to do what is best to maintain its natural condition, when it is required to perform contrary to its basic function, mental turmoil and distress result.

Each irritation of the body transmits its own electrical impulse to the brain. With so many signals entering the body, the brain is engulfed in a storm of activity. To protect its integrity, the brain must channel these impulses to where they won't interfere with its proper functioning. They are sent into the subconscious to be stored as background information.

Each of these electrical impulses is minor alone, but when combined, they become a major source of distress. They build in the subconscious with no outlet for their combining energies until the emotions come into play.

Since the emotions use the subconscious part of the brain to compute, with the help of reason, recall past experiences and come to conclusions to prepare a proper reaction to a stimulus, they are negatively influenced by the irritations that have been transmitted by the body.

The affected emotional responses may not be unnatural on an obvious level. They may be too subtle to notice. For instance, constriction of the waist by a tight belt will adversely affect digestion, impede the efficient flow of blood through the waist region and cause generalized physical discomfort. These distresses are obvious. The constriction also creates a less apparent reaction: distorting emotional response.

A common source of irritation can actually cause an emotional over-reaction to a minor stimulus. A few of the negative responses, irritability, anger, and frustration, can result from the constriction of the body. This may not be as obvious a reaction as subjective physical distress, but it is just as real and perhaps more *unhealthy*.

Man's freedom to move, to feel, to contact his environment with all of his physical senses is his natural condition. Clothing is an artificial, unhealthy restriction of that freedom.

By sending negative signals to the brain, physical irritation causes unhealthy emotional responses. Even a minor constriction of body freedom can create physical misery, and thereby create distress in the other two spheres.

POOR HEALTH

Physical illness seems to be an inescapable part of life. Very few people can claim that they have never been sick. Most of us suffer at least a minor illness such as a cold, the flu, or an upset stomach occasionally. Besides the minor illness most of us have once in a while, there are some people who suffer chronically from headaches, indigestion, insomnia, and other such nagging pains. Some people contract more serious diseases, even catastrophic ones which sometimes end their lives.

Physical illness, however minor, poses a serious threat to our well being in more than just the physical sphere of our body. If you have ever had a cold or the flu, you know all too well how the illness makes you feel. Besides the nagging aches, pains and general physical discomfort, your mind is fuzzy and your thinking is unclear.

Our body and emotions are intimately related. The three spheres interconnect and directly influence each other. Physical illness, a real conscious distress, has a powerful, obvious relationship to our emotions.

Physical survival is the most basic and powerful of our instincts. It overrides all other considerations. Survival means the continuation of the species and the success of man's continued existence upon this planet. Every reaction of the being is directed toward the ultimate end of perpetuating physical survival.

When pain occurs, it signifies a major threat to survival. The brain, working at its most basic level, *must* take corrective action. That action will be strong, dramatic and instant. It could range from simply numbing some of the nerve endings to make the pain more bearable to demanding unconsciousness to protect itself from being overwhelmed by the pain's intensity. It is the ultimate reaction, *the* most important.

Both major and minor physical illness may be accompanied by pain. Physical distress always signals a warning to the brain that demands corrective action. That action will ensure survival. When the brain is compelled into what it conceives as a possible danger, it acts with a tremendous amount of power to protect itself. Since every action must have an equal and opposite reaction, it should not be surprising that this power translates itself into other actions.

The opposite reaction in the emotional sphere can range from temporary confusion to absolute calm, to apathy or violent rage. Its direction can only be generally predicted. The emotional reaction to pain will be as severe or as moderate as the distress that causes it.

The list of man's illnesses is seemingly endless. It can range from common aches and pains to pneumonia, measles, diabetes, coronary distress, epilepsy, and so on. The relative severity of physical distress goes from bare minimum to termination. It makes little difference how serious the distress is since the brain is compelled to react to life-threatening stimuli in a very violent, passionate way. It is only the *final form* of the reaction that will be in relative intensity to the stimulus. The *process* is the same for minor and severe illness.

Disease and poor condition certainly cause the largest portion of physical distress, but another major contributor to poor health is inferior hygiene. Not keeping the body clean means that bacteria and other organisms have a breeding ground. An irregular program of personal hygiene can also lead to a negative self-image. Although that is not a cause of physical distress *per se,* the discomfort does create problems with the emotions. For all of these reasons, hygiene becomes a major determining factor in how we get along in the physical sphere.

Physical trouble converts irritation into action by causing an immediate, forceful response by the brain. Because of the interrelationships of the three spheres of being, poor health is a direct cause of distress.

<u>UNHEALTHY SEXUAL INHIBITIONS</u>

Since survival is our most powerful instinct, it is logical that sex should be only slightly less potent. The ultimate objective of all our natural reactions is the enhancement of life, and sex is a means to that end. Procreation is the method for survival of the species and for its continuation and growth. Because procreation is affected through sexual relations, its natural necessity is obvious.

As an adjunct to reproduction, sex is also fun. Intense sensual pleasure, joy and consequent release of tension comes through intimate contact with another person. The pleasure of sex means that procreation will occur often because man will indulge his appetite often. The pure gratification of sexual release helps to insure the survival of man upon the planet.

Although sexual encounters are natural and usually healthy, our expression is often inhibited by social conditioning and moral codes of conduct. The religious view of morality holds that certain acts are either "good" or "bad", but if you substitute "healthy" for good and "unhealthy" for bad, the fallacy of some moral principles is clear.

For instance, sex out of wedlock is usually considered immoral behavior by religious standards. But substituting "unhealthy" for "immoral" makes the statement untrue. There is nothing necessarily *unhealthy* about sex out of wedlock. The sexual instinct is *natural* and having sexual relations with a consenting partner is *healthy*. Whether it occurs out of wedlock is irrelevant. The moral command against sex in this case *inhibits* healthy expression.

Most moral codes are universal in their condemnation of sex between partners of the same gender. Here again, the sexual expression is natural. Simply because the partner is of the same gender does not necessarily make that expression *unhealthy*. If the partner is consenting, if he/she has a positive attitude about his/her sexual relations (pure passion *is* a positive reason.), if his/her feeling of well being is enhanced because of their encounter, his/her sexual expression is healthy. If it is not *unhealthy*, neither is it *immoral*.

Certainly all moral dictates are *not* unhealthy. Again, by substitution, many of them are true and life enhancing. The moral command against murder, for instance, would say that murder is unhealthy, *and it is*. Since it ends the survival of another human being, murder is the ultimate life destructive act. An action is just as *unhealthy* if we *cause* it to someone else. It's as if we do it to ourselves.

The fallacies of many other moral commandments are easy to demonstrate by substituting their wording with words that relate to the way things are and not as they *should be*. The inhibitions of our healthy expressions are undisguised.

Whenever we inhibit our healthy expressions, we stifle our natural condition and our well being suffers. By using moralistic dictates of our sexual actions or by *not* expressing ourselves because of a fallacious taboo against it, we inhibit healthy life enhancing reactions. Just because we don't perform a healthy expression doesn't necessarily make it *unhealthy*. Our natural condition is an absolute freedom of choice. So if we choose <u>not</u> to express our sexuality in a certain way, that is our natural right. But, if we don't express our sexuality because we are inhibited either by fallacious external moral codes or by internal negative attitudes, we are acting *contrary to our well being*. By accepting the inhibition, we have made our reactions *not* to express our sexuality *unhealthy*.

The inhibition of healthy sexual expression has dire consequences. If there is denial of the body's real need for release or for the desired experience of pleasure, sexual tension builds up in the body. This tension can cause severe physical distress that affects the emotions.

Inhibition of a healthy sexual expression can lead to negative emotional perspectives such as depression, insomnia, anger and even irritability.

None of these actions will *always* come about. The physical distress may translate itself into a less obvious, delayed emotional reaction. Worse than an obvious distortion of emotional responses, the delayed reaction will distort emotional expression so subtly it may go unnoticed for a long time. Regardless of the exact nature of the negative reaction to physical frustration, unhealthy sexual inhibitions lead directly to emotional and spiritual distress.

Nothing exists from whose nature
Some effect does not follow.
—Benedict Spinoza

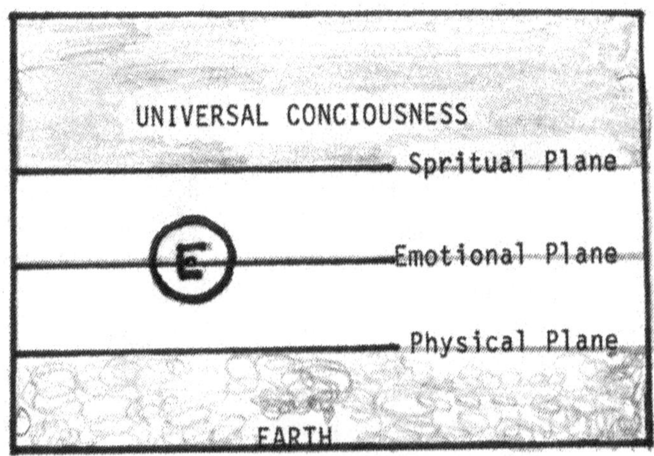

ILLUSTRATION 6

EMOTIONAL CAUSES

We've just seen how physical distress can adversely influence the other two spheres of being. Each sphere is intimately connected with the other two.

Similar to the emotional effects caused by physical distress, and vice versa, unhealthy emotions can cause physical disturbance. Unexplained itches and pains, and all sorts of ailments are classified by science into a special category of disorders that constitute "psychosomatic disease."

Although the magnitude of emotional effects upon physical health is not fully understood by traditional science, it is a well-accepted fact that the two spheres share an intimate cause-and-effect relationship. There are as many emotional causes of physical illness as there are causes purely of the body.

Again, because of their strong interrelationship, emotional disturbance also creates spiritual distress. Since the third sphere of being exerts a more forceful and much subtler influence over our well being, any disturbance of emotional well being is very serious.

<u>PHOBIAS</u>

A major source of emotional disturbance involves a conditioned reaction that is incorporated into the thought process, therefore causing distortion. Its influence is as subtle as its origin.

Phobias are intense, irrational fears that overpower logic and cause reactions that are out of proportion to the stimulus. The source of fear, the original reaction that later becomes magnified and distorted into a phobia, was necessary and healthy when it was first called up.

Let me illustrate. Say a child is suddenly and violently involved in a fire. His natural survival instinct is to run out of the burning building to save his life, to avoid imminent death by fire. His instinct that demands escape is motivated by necessary, healthy fear.

We have fears for our own protection. When we are confronted by an anti-survival situation, an occurrence that somehow threatens our well being, our instinctive reaction is repulsion, to get away from it, not allow it to cause us harm.

Fears are powerful, positive reactions to negative life-threatening events. When we are born, our instincts are directed toward survival. Whenever we encounter a situation that might harm us, we react naturally and strongly to it. We experience fear.

Right after we start investigating our environment, we are immediately faced with survival threatening incidents. For example, a flame from a stove, electrical wires, or dangerously high places from which we could fall cause fear.

Each new situation is fed into our subconscious. The nature of the situation is recorded along with information on why it is life threatening, why our reaction was healthy or why we should react similarly to a similar stimulus in the future.

By conditioning and slowly learning which events, situations and objects threaten our survival, our subconscious memories of instinctive reactions become a source of healthy life enhancing fears that are destined to aid our physical survival.

Some fears come about because of our instinct for *emotional* survival as well as physical. We need emotional survival to enhance our lives and to improve our well being. By discovering attitudes and situations that threaten our emotional survival, we slowly add these fears to our subconscious store.

These pro-survival fears are natural and healthy. They are positive reactions to negative stimuli. Because emotional reactions are influenced by a variety of subconscious memories and anxieties, our natural fears can become distorted.

The instance of the child in the fire is a good example.

His is a purely hypothetical case, but it illustrates the principle succinctly.

The child's instinct and the facts surrounding the burning building have been stored and categorized in his mind. He has formed a natural, healthy fear of fire.

If he is threatened in a similar manner again later in life, this fear will help protect him from injury.

However, a phobia could develop. Let's say that the child sees his mother die in a second fire. His instinctual reaction will be toward survival, to escape. The trauma of seeing his mother burn is too severe for his mind to handle. The emotional experience colors his natural fear, making it unhealthy.

One possible phobic reaction to this traumatic experience would be for the child's subconscious to channel the memory to a remote part of his information banks where it will be invisible and where its presence won't affect his conscious mental functioning. By removing the irritation, the child's emotional survival is enhanced. He can function better without the traumatic experience influencing his everyday thinking.

The child may remember the fire. He may even remember seeing his mother die, but the real intense emotional trauma of his reaction will remain deep in his subconscious where it cannot become a permanent disability to his continued emotional well being.

Another example would be that someday the child encounters a similar circumstance involving a match. It looks the same, it has a flame and heat, and he knows instinctively that it is dangerous and could be life-threatening. His mind reaches into stored memories to determine a proper reaction. There it finds the healthy fear of fire. Suddenly there is the associated, intense emotional trauma of his mother's violent death. The two reactions mix and a serious phobia is created. In over-reaction to the circumstance, equating fire with death, he goes into a panic and flees to escape the threat of the match's flame.

This example of the creation of a phobia is fictional and is arguably extreme, but it does show the inner workings of an important process. When healthy fears and traumatic memories mix, when they are equated by the mind as being *the same event*, the instinctual reaction is distorted by non-related facts.

Most of us have many fears that we've learned in the course of our lives. These fears are mostly healthy and life enhancing. When an otherwise healthy, physical fear is associated with a related trauma, however minor, the information becomes confused. Fire is associated with death. Fire is a part of death. Fire *is* death. The equation dangerously distorts the truth. Our healthy fear has been turned into an unhealthy phobia.

A seemingly insignificant event in a person's life may be at the root of an irrational fear. As an example, a child falls down the stairs of his home. During the fall, before he finally strikes the floor, he sees and feels a thousand different images. The impression of sound, sight, smell, and feeling occurred *while he was falling*. He isn't consciously aware of a single one after the fall, but they have been neatly stored in his subconscious for future reference.

His fear of falling was natural and healthy. It aided his physical survival. Someday, far removed by time and place from those stairs and high places, he suffers a severe panic attack, an undefined fear reaction to an unknown stimulus. All the man knows is that he was sitting in a hotel room, the doorbell rang and he was suddenly, irrationally terrified. There is no logical explanation for his extreme reaction. At least none of which he is *aware*.

If he could see into his subconscious, the man's irrational fear reaction has a clear detectable cause. When he was falling down the stairs, one of the sounds he heard was a strange bell. It was one he had never heard before. Maybe it was a sound from the television downstairs. He couldn't consciously recall hearing it, but the sound had been filed away in his subconscious during the fall. The doorbell in the hotel room was similar, and the sound triggered an association of memories, causing his irrational panic.

His mental process matched the memories, tied the sound to the fear of falling and equated them. The doorbell set off a chain of mental events that made the unusual sound a related part of the incident that had *originally* threatened his survival.

In every waking moment we are barraged by literally millions of perceptions of our environment. If we're walking down a city street to the movies, our attention is focused upon what is in front of us. As we walk, every piece of scenery we pass, each sight out of the corners of our eyes, the sounds, smells, and all of the sensory information around us, is recorded in subconscious memory. We are rarely aware of the wealth of information we perceive every moment because our attention is elsewhere. To illustrate the point, sometime just stop yourself somewhere and look around. Listen, sniff, touch, and see what has just been filed away in storage. You might be surprised.

We all associate various *parts* of an event in our memory, too. If we feel good about walking, we associate the beneficial feeling with the physical act of walking. Likewise, we make mental associations between other occurrences to sort them out and to keep them in some logical order.

When our mind associates a severe, traumatic occurrence with a fear, that fear is intensified. The more severe the emotional association, the more out of proportion the fear reaction becomes. Conversely, if the emotional association is relatively mild, so will be the reaction. The associations in our mind are not the problem. The problem comes when we fail to recognize that the associations are not *necessarily* related. The child's mother dying in a fire is not *necessarily* related to falling. When mental associations become too entangled or when their separateness becomes sameness, distorted responses result.

It does not necessarily follow that B is a *result* of A. They may be related. They may have both been present at the same time, but if A is a fear and B is an incidental occurrence (something that just *accidentally happened* at the same time) then B may not be a direct effect of A's cause. The association could be illogical.

Associations are necessary to maintain the integrity of the memory and to make retrieval of information more systematic. They set up a method of classifying data according to relationships with each other. The association of traumatic experience with natural, healthy reaction is fallacious and leads to trouble.

In the case of the child, if his mother had not died, and if he had instead associated fire with burning wood, his reaction to the match may have been very different. Instead of becoming emotionally upset, he may have made a coldly logical decision about his fears. He may have been extremely cautious being near the stimulus, but he wouldn't panic.

The man's reaction to the strange sound is similar. If, instead of falling, the doorbell had been associated with the arrival of a favorite relative, his reaction might have been one of joy or happy expectation. Of course, if falling had been associated only with the odor of fresh paint, the man wouldn't have had any appreciable reaction to the doorbell. The fallacious association would not have worked.

When we consciously allow ourselves to make decisions based on what we intuitively know to be illogical associations, we are creating a possible phobic reaction. If we are not already aware of the fallacies, by a deep introspection and an honest appraisal of subconscious memories, we can easily see them.

Phobias can be such varied things as irrational fears to certain *types* of people or an intense fear of a particular *color*. They are irrational associations of people, objects, or situations with fear. The fear and the memory are *actually separate*. By combining them, irrational fear of high places (acrophobia), the fear of water (hydrophobia), and the fear of being alone (monophobia) are created.

There are many people under treatment by psychiatrists for common, though severe, phobias. There are many that have an irrational, crippling fear of elevators. They panic when inside one. Others have phobias about flying. Subconsciously, all of these panic reactions are the result of fallacious associations and they are common occurrences.

Since phobic reactions have such a serious impact on emotional equilibrium, a disturbance is set up in the physical sphere of being and distorted spiritual reactions are magnified.

Any disturbance in one sphere adversely affects the others. Phobias directly influence first and third sphere activity and are a major cause of distress.

<u>UNHEALTHY STEREOTYPES</u>

As with phobias, stereotypes are also caused by association. While they are not, *per se,* unhealthy, the associations related to stereotypes are sometimes fallacious. They often cause emotional disturbance.

A stereotype, very simply, is a preconceived expectation, a way of thinking we know what will happen before it actually does. When we meet a new situation and already know how we *expect* it to turn out, we are often operating by stereotype.

Assume that a woman hears a story told to her over and over by her father. He says husbands are no-good bastards and they will leave her barefoot and pregnant without a "thank you." That is certainly a stereotype. The father says that *all husbands* will react the same, and in this case, irresponsibly and egocentrically with no regard for the woman.

The model is obviously fallacious. *All* members of *any group*, including husbands, don't act the same. The woman who hears this stereotypical horror story the first time sees the patent falsehood it perpetuates. The second time, she will still see it. After the thousandth time her father repeats the fallacy, and although the woman still realizes deep inside that the story *is* a fallacy, the absurdity will have been reinforced by constant repetition. It doesn't sound *quite* so silly anymore. Not true, of course, she thinks privately. But then again, not *too* farfetched. True or not, the stereotype is stored in her memory under possible descriptions of a husband.

By the time she marries, the woman isn't even aware of the stereotype she has buried in her subconscious. She loves her husband dearly and knows he's being fair and honest with her.

As the years go by, the woman and her husband still love each other, but the zest has gone out of their marriage. They don't talk anymore and they seem to be interested in different things. They start arguing more and more.

One day she and her husband have a heated argument. She gets angry and yells, "You no-good bastard!" When they both cool down, she apologizes, and they make up. Slowly, as she reflects on the argument, she remembers the stereotype. I said he was a no-good bastard, she thinks. He's not, of course, but if he is....

The woman's husband probably won't leave her if he's stayed this long, so her concern won't necessarily be justified. The stereotype she incorporated into her subconscious has exerted a subtle influence on her marriage since she associated "husband" with the expected disastrous outcome. She could *cause* her concern to become reality.

The stereotype of egocentric, uncaring husband was deep in the woman's subconscious, so she set up an unconscious *expectation*. Every time her husband did something, the woman unconsciously associated it with the stereotypical behavior. Of course, her expectation was never obvious. She was never actually *aware* of comparing her husband to an unconscious expectation. The subtle influence was there all the while, causing her to see her husband in a distorted light. The *expectation* had set up an artificial barrier to their spontaneous relationship.

A learned stereotype sets up a fallacious expectation of someone's action to or with us. We have already visualized the situation through the stereotype and *know* how it will end. We've already met, or heard about, this *type* of person. Obviously, *this* is how he's going to act.

Whether a person or situation actually fulfills the expectation, the stereotype nonetheless exerts a powerful influence over our reactions. At every turn, we are already prepared for what we *expect* as opposed to reacting to the stimulus *spontaneously*.

If you look into your own mind, you can find many stereotypes sitting idly in your subconscious just waiting to be put to use. They are all basically the same. The way stereotypes are constructed, their imagery even *appears* absurd. "_______________ always _____________ ", "All _____________ are _____________", "_____________ should _____________." These are stereotype concepts. Just fill in the blanks with your own people, situations or expectations.

There is very little on this planet that is *always* any particular way. *All* of any group is rarely *identical.* There are some things we are told we *should* do that are actually *unhealthy.* With the unlimited diversity of people, an *absolute* statement about anything dealing with people is usually fallacious.

The Eastern concept of *yin/yang* relates to absolutism saying that things are either *all* this or *all* that. *Yin* in this concept represents the positive such as day, heaven, white, purity, and beneficial qualities. *Yang* is its opposite, representing the negative side, such as night, hell, black, evil, and the malevolent qualities. It is a matter of practicality that either *yin* or *yang* might exist independently. In dealing with others, and ourselves, there is very little that is either *completely* black or white, all *yin* or all *yang.*

Most things in life are *degrees* of *yin/yang.* Just about all of our interpersonal experience lies somewhere between *totally* positive and *totally* negative. Most events we encounter have a little of each. Some may be mostly positive with a *little* negative. Others may be *mostly* negative and *slightly* positive. Most of our life is spent with some combination of *yin* and *yang,* or *yin/yang.*

This explanation is necessarily brief. The whole concept of *yin/yang* embodies an entire philosophy that is a way of looking at the world. It is more complicated than presented in this condensation, but how *yin/yang* is involved in our daily lives comes through in spite of the over-simplification.

The word "healthy" is not an absolute in interpreting stereotypes. Just because it sets up an expectation does not *necessarily* make the stereotype *un*healthy. It depends entirely on the context.

The stereotype, "Men *should* like sports," for example, becomes silly when it is interpreted to state, "Men who like sports are *healthy.*" Just because a man *likes* something doesn't mean he gets the benefit. The stereotype sets up a fallacious expectation that if a man likes sports, it is necessarily beneficial to him. He could just as easily be physically distressed by his fondness of sports.

On the other hand, the stereotype, "People *should* respect each other." is true and beneficial. When it states, "Respecting other people is *healthy*." it demonstrates a life enhancing attribute. By respecting each other we acknowledge our common humanity, our natural right to individual freedom and our right to be treated as equals. Contrary to the first example, this stereotype creates a *healthy* expectation, one that aids our mutual survival. The first example was *yang*, this one *yin*. Together they form *yin/yang*, which is a combination.

If the above stereotypes sound reminiscent of a moral code, there is a very good reason. Moral dictates *are* stereotypes. They set up an expectation that obedience to them is *necessarily* healthy. It becomes obvious through interpretation that while some moral dictates are truly beneficial and healthy, others seriously imperil our well being. Some moral commandments are downright unhealthy. They are not *necessarily* either healthy or unhealthy. It depends on the case.

In the same way that we can see the fallacy of some moral commandments, we can analyze any other stereotype. By seeing the statement in relation to the enhancement or subjugation of health, its relative merit becomes clear. That an action is *healthy* is the most logical reason for *doing it*. If it is *unhealthy*, that is a bonafide reason for *avoiding it*. Looking at stereotypes in this context, interpretation is simplified.

Racism, sexism, elitism, and most-ism's are beliefs that some group of people, ideas, and thoughts, are necessarily inferior to another. "*All* blacks are inferior", "*All* gays are sick", "Labor *should* vote Democratic", "Women *belong* in the home", are fallacious stereotypes that encourage, in fact, reward unhealthy negative expectations by *dividing* divergent groups.

All stereotypes presuppose one requirement. The person who has the expectation *cannot* have an open mind. It is a plain impossibility to have a *lack of preconceptions* if a stereotype is going to effective.

By setting up expected reactions, stereotypes color emotional responses with preconceptions so that they are no longer natural or spontaneous. The reactions are being negatively influenced.

Because of their strong emotional effect, the distortions created by stereotypes reflect in the other spheres of being and become a major cause of distress.

<u>DESTRUCTIVE LOVE/HATE</u>

Just as in the case of phobias, stereotypes or nearly any other area of interpersonal relationships, love/hate is not *necessarily* healthy or unhealthy.

The slash between the words "love" and "hate" has more significance than just eliminating the modification "and/or." It symbolizes the real practical *similarity* of those emotions.

Love is directed *toward*, hate *against* an object. They are both relatively strong emotional reactions to emotional survival. Love is directed *toward* a beneficial life enhancing situation. Hate is directed *against* a potentially anti-survival occurrence. In these respects, they are similar.

The fundamental difference between love and hate is only in their *direction* of force. Although love is directed *toward* and hate *against*, they are actually the *same* emotional reaction with equal intensity though they appear on the surface to be opposites.

From an instinctual standpoint, both love and hate are strong emotional responses to a survival question. If the question is positive and increases our well being or our contentment, we respond with love. If it is a life-threatening situation instead, we react strongly with hate, an emotional defense against threatened destruction.

Love is oftentimes a healthy reaction, but so is hate. If either is a spontaneous reaction to a stimulus, positive *or* negative, and the reaction aids in the end goal of survival, they are *equally* healthy.

For example, a man loves his brother. They see each other as adding positive energy to their individual lives. Since their reactions are *toward* each other and they each add to the other's well being, their love is healthy, a *constructive* influence.

However, if one brother's reaction to the other is to ridicule him and make him into a menial servant of the other's emotional needs without *adding* anything to the relationship, only *taking* from him, one brother's love for the other can be *unhealthy*. The love is misplaced and misdirected *toward* his brother's negative behavior instead of *against* it.

On the other hand, should one brother's reaction to the same negative stimulus be *against* emotional subservience and in favor of survival, the properly directed *hate* is just as healthy as the love in the first instance.

Love/hate is not either healthy or unhealthy, but either pro or anti-survival. If the *result* of the response *benefits* personal well being, it is healthy. If it *adversely* affects emotional equilibrium, it is unhealthy. The *direction* of the response is irrelevant. It is its *result*, its enhancement or reduction of well being that is important.

With expansion of the *yin/yang* principle, it becomes clear that most interpersonal relationships involve both love *and* hate at the same time. Very few of our reactions are properly directed either totally *toward* or *against* a stimulus. Most of our reactions are a mixture.

That mixture is healthy of itself. If we can recognize that our reaction is related to a single attractive/repulsive issue we are usually able to realize that most of our emotional content is love or hate while there is simultaneously a very subtle influence of hate or love. Our reaction is simply love or hate.

The general term love/hate embodies a wide range of emotions. They range from pure love, which is *totally* toward, to like, which is less forceful, but still *toward* the stimulus, to apathy which is a lack of *any* emotion, to dislike, which is mostly *against,* to pure hate, which is a *maximum intensity* against, at the other end. Between these lie a myriad of other emotions with which we are involved most often. They are responses with widely varying intensities and complexities.

If love/hate results in our enhanced survival, and if our well being is increased, our emotional, physical, and spiritual durability strengthens. It is healthy and beneficial. If love/hate is <u>not</u> in proper reaction to the stimulus or if it is based instead upon misunderstanding, or if the stimulus is incorrectly associated in the mind with facts that are, in fact, *unrelated* to the stimulus, the reaction is *unhealthy, destructive*, and leads to serious emotional disturbance.

Because it sets up turmoil in the emotional sphere of being, destructive love/hate is a direct cause of distress.

<u>NONPRODUCTIVE FANTASY LIFE</u>

The material world deals on a very real, concrete level. It is concerned with practicality, reason, and logical reactions. Even our emotional dealings with our material environment function on this lower, basic level.

The material world is very taxing on our finite store of energy. Physical, emotional, and spiritual interactions drain our energy supply. To function at their optimum capacity, each sphere must react with *full power*. They work well even when tired, but when they are relaxed, they work *better*.

Sleep fulfills this need for rest, at least partially. Even during relative quiet, the spheres continue their functions though with a reduced zeal. The heart beats to maintain necessary body activity. The spirit has an opportunity to more easily contact the higher forces, and the emotions continue their process of sifting through information received during waking hours.

Our dreams offer an unconscious glimpse into our mental functioning. Unrelated facts are weighed and sorted by the mind while they are interpreted by the emotions. The result is a short series of words and pictures, a graphic presentation of our mental activity replete with wide screen and Dolby stereo.

By dealing fully and continuously with reality, the emotions are in even more need of relaxation than the other spheres. They need some kind of relief valve for protection. Enter Fantasy!

Fantasy is the contradiction of reality. It is a purely mental world where conclusions don't have to proceed logically from assumptions, where anything can be done without regard to reason. It's a world where *all things are possible.*

In fantasy we can experience absolute freedom without the restraint of materialistic rules. We can let our imaginations go wild. If we like, we can talk intelligently to the man in the moon and then turn around and resume the business of The Presidency. We can throw a ball into the air and watch it go up and up through outer space to infinity. It need not obey the laws of gravity. We can sail the globe in fantasy installments and create a detailed adventure scenario without having to travel. In short, we can envision any possible, *or impossible,* circumstance and fully enjoy the experience.

Creative imagination calls for using the mind's innate ability to visualize what is reality and deal with it *as if it were.* Through imagination we can construct a private "New Republic" of our own and build fantasies in, around and through it. We have the ability to create our own make-believe world inside our fantasies.

The imaginative creation *is* our world. Nobody can see what goes on in our mind. Only we know our fantasies. They are *completely private.* Fantasies can rarely be analyzed. Their images will "not compute." Since fantasies violate all the rules of logical thinking, even their perception is unintelligible to anyone else.

Since our fantasies are private, they are the only place where we can flagrantly violate all the rules without retaliation. The vice-president of the bank can safely tell off his boss without fear of losing his job. The president of the bank can play the violin in Carnegie Hall without worrying what his employees might think. The writer can give his acceptance speech for the Pulitzer Prize to an envying crowd of his peers. We can *safely* fulfill our dreams.

These are healthy fantasies. Even such seemingly harmful fantasies as tying and torturing an imagined enemy, planning a daring robbery, even masturbating in a department store window during Christmas rush are healthy because of the relief valve effect. If we can deal with frustrations, anger and fear through fantasy, it is often easier to handle. The possibilities of acting out the situation in the real world are lessened because the intense emotions associated with those fantasies are likewise lessened.

If we deal with controversial, even life-threatening situations in our fantasies, shouldn't they sometimes be *unhealthy* and *destructive* to our well being? About the only times it becomes a real problem is when the mind ceases to be able to distinguish between fantasy and reality and the two are confused. An example of this is when there is severe psychosis, irrational thinking, or when a person acts out his fantasies, when he performs in the material world an unhealthy act that he conceived in fantasy. Even here, the fantasy isn't at fault, only the incidental action is unhealthy. In this situation, the fantasy serves as an unwitting *healthy means* to an unfortunate *un*healthy end.

"All work and no play make Jack a dull boy" is an old truism. By giving them a break from having to deal with complicated reality, creative imagination allows the emotions to enjoy themselves. They are free to play with the mind, to miscalculate, deceive, and act illogically. Being able to be illogical is pure recreation to the emotions, a vacation from reality.

A further benefit of an active, productive fantasy life is the enhancement of our ability to more faithfully perform appropriate emotional reactions, to respond more accurately and more spontaneously.

It is obvious that a healthy fantasy life is beneficial to the *total being*. It is easy to see that a lack of an adequate fantasy life is a hindrance to optimum performance.

While an insufficient fantasy life is not necessarily an unhealthy problem, by making it more difficult to sort problems, to fully comprehend and deal with stress, a lack of imaginative fantasy can cause misery in all three spheres of being.

Great men are they who see that
spiritual is stronger than any
material force; that thoughts rule
the world.
—Ralph Waldo Emerson

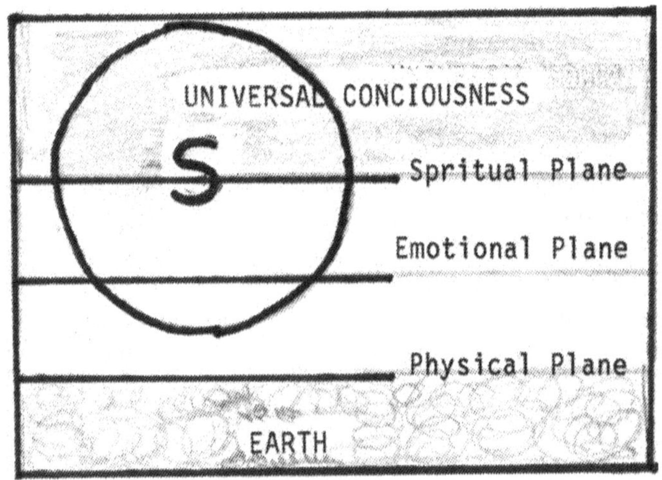

ILLUSTRATION 7

SPIRITUAL CAUSES

Since the third sphere of being concerns our highest purpose, disturbances of a spiritual nature exert a more pervasive influence on the lower spheres. The spiritual function of being is by far of much higher magnitude with a consequently greater significance.

Because the final goal is of such vital importance, the necessity of spiritual purity so great, any third sphere disturbance is necessarily severe.

POOR CONCENTRATION/ COMPREHENSION/REALIZATION

The mind functions on a higher level of complexity than the body. It is emotional on a higher level than the mind. Those functions become more complex, dealing with abstract ideas and intelligible reactions.

Since function is directly related to severity of disturbance, emotional distress is necessarily more damaging than it would be in the lowest sphere. Likewise, spiritual function works on the highest, most complex level and suffers more intensely from any disturbance. When its purpose of superphysical communication is hampered, spiritual distress translates itself into much more subtle, overpowering influences in the lower two spheres of being.

A prevalent cause of spiritual distress has to do primarily with the non-recognition of third sphere purpose. By not being fully aware of its high nature, how it functions and how we can help it to achieve its goal, we severely hamper spiritual growth. If we don't understand where it's going, we can't speed it toward its destination.

The esoteric functions of the spiritual sphere of being bears a resemblance to the material world in some respects. If we keep our car in good repair, add oil to its engine as necessary and generally help it to run better, the car will be better able to serve its purpose of transporting us. Spiritual functioning deals on a completely different level, above, *beyond* the material world, but it is very similar to the car. If we nourish it, protect it, and help it, the spirit will be better able to achieve its ultimate goal.

The spiritual sphere of being is called by many names. Sometimes it is called "soul," "psyche," "essence," "supernatural world," and many different words to describe the same high function. Spirit is a psychic receptor, a residing place for the soul. It is our essence, what we *are*. It deals with a supernatural world, a world beyond the material dimension.

Through the traditional Eastern description of our relationship to the highest level of being, the workings of the spiritual sphere become easier to understand.

Visualize a pool of clear water. Each microscopic drop is identical to every other drop of water in the pool. Each has the same characteristics, components, the same basic nature, and the same molecules. Each is a *microcosm of the whole*.

If we dip a cupful of water out of the pool, the water in the cup takes on a separate existence. The cup has effectively isolated part of the water from the pool. Even though the water in the cup is physically separated from that in the pool, they share identical characteristics. In spite of their separation, the molecules remain the same.

The cup represents our physical body. The water symbolizes our spiritual being. Although our spirit, like the water in the cup, has an existence apart from Universal Consciousness, the pool of spiritual essence, our higher sphere, is a *microcosm of it*. The individual spirit is still a part of the whole.

The dimension of Universal Consciousness is the substance of being. All that is, or ever has been, will coexist there. Individual energies merge into an infinite whole. Everything that is conceivable to our minds is embodied there:

the pure essence of all thought, material, reality, and fantasy. Universal Consciousness is *everything simultaneously*. It *IS*!

When we begin our travel through this physical existence, we have a body in which to house our spiritual being: the cup that contains the water. In the beginning, when we are physically born, our spiritual sphere has a bare minimum of energy, rather like *diluted* water.

Each experience we have during our material existence carries with it its own unique energy. If the experience is life enhancing, it is *positive* in charge. If the experience is destructive, anti-survival, it is *negative*. Every experience contributes its particular energy to our spiritual supply. If positive in nature, the experience *adds* power to our third sphere. If it is negative, it *removes* some.

By constantly adding to our spiritual store, we approach the ultimate goal of spiritual perfection. Throughout our physical existence we are adding or subtracting spiritual energy until, in our final existence, we achieve maximum input.

The law of Karma influences our spiritual growth. Among other effects, this mystical principle of cause-and-effect demonstrates that every spiritual action has an equal and opposite reaction. If we *give* positive energy, we will later *receive* it. The same applies to the negative. We reap what we sow, as it were. The success of our physical existence is determined by the degree of our progress, by the amount of positive or negative energy we collect. We start our next physical existence at the point of spiritual development (amount of energy) where we left off in our last life. The more positive energy we have in our spiritual sphere at the new beginning, the less we have to add to achieve perfection, the less complicated and traumatic will be our coming physical existence.

At the end of its material journey our spiritual being is liberated from the body. Like the water is poured out of the cup to rejoin its nature, our spiritual sphere merges back into Universal Consciousness.

When our spiritual being, our essence, once again requires physical experience to add more psychic energy to its store, the search for spiritual perfection begins anew. When we finally achieve that ultimate goal, when our spiritual being attains maximum energy, our need for further manifestations on the material plane is ended. When our final physical existence is ended, our spiritual being merges into Universal Consciousness completely. It becomes *ONE* with *ALL*.

We no longer *need* physical experience once we achieve spiritual perfection and we can rejoin Universal Consciousness for eternity. If we so choose, we can manifest again on the material plane for our own reasons. This decision becomes the ultimate *freedom of choice*.

It is possible to lessen the need for multiple physical existence, to accelerate the process of achieving spiritual perfection. By building maximum energy during this existence, we can end our need for further experience in the physical world and become one with Universal Consciousness, where the total *being is*.

By contacting Universal Consciousness directly through our spiritual link, we can tap the source of spiritual power and, through it, channel that energy and siphon it into our spiritual sphere of being.

Without the added positive energy, our spiritual involvement would slow and perfection would take more than the present physical existence. By annexing large amounts of positive energy to our spiritual sphere, we can greatly assist in the goal of achieving spiritual perfection. By attaining that goal, we end the necessity for further manifestations.

When we no longer need physical experience, we attain oneness with Universal Consciousness and the absolute freedom of choice. Without the addition of positive energy during the present manifestation, this goal would involve much unnecessary suffering. Because of the Law of Karma, some beings are not yet fully developed enough to realize that spiritual growth without suffering is possible.

Realization is the first step in accelerating spiritual growth. When we have total intuitive wisdom, as opposed to lower level *intellectual understanding*, we have made partial contact with Universal Consciousness. We receive intimate information of esoteric functioning of the spiritual sphere, knowledge we would never obtain through logical reasoning. Realization amounts to drawing upon Universal Consciousness for help in the attainment of perfection.

Concentration assists Realization. By being able to focus all of our mental powers upon becoming Realized, the first step is taken. We can exclude all but one thought and direct our entire attention onto that single issue. If our thought process can focus its vast store of psychic energy in one controlled orientation, more power is concentrated upon the single concept than if our energy is unfocused and directed at a number of divergent issues.

Without effective concentration, Realization is difficult, if not altogether impossible. Further, concentration is necessary for implementing some other cures to spiritual distress. Poor concentration seriously impedes our success in accelerating spiritual growth.

Likewise, without full comprehension of spiritual functioning, Realization is impossible. If we have no idea what we're looking for or how to recognize Universal Consciousness when we *do* make contact, our success is doomed. With poor comprehension, even with solid *intellectual understanding*, focusing all our energy will not be effective. We must first know our intended *direction*.

Poor concentration/comprehension/Realization, because of the complex needs for forceful direction of our psychic energies, causes spiritual distress and thus directly harms all spheres of being simultaneously.

INSUFFICIENT PSYCHIC PERCEPTION/AWARENESS

The lower spheres of being deal with differing levels of the material plane, visible reality. Physical reactions come from gross experiences of the body: pain, pleasure, tension and calm. Emotional experiences are basically electrochemical reactions to physical stimuli, distress in response to discomfort, joy in response to pleasure. Even emotional reactions such as sorrow, love/hate, ecstasy are complex in origin, but primarily electrochemical in nature.

Third sphere reactions come from a higher level, from non-material information which we receive through interaction in another dimension, one which has no parallel in material existence.

There are five basic physical senses that describe the bulk of the ways we receive information from our environment. Sight, taste, touch, hearing and smell convey our perceptions to our mind and emotional sphere for translation into appropriate reaction.

The physical senses and their related emotional responses concern our *material* environment. A sixth sense, psychic perception, operates through the third spiritual sphere of being.

Because there are probably more than the five physical senses mentioned and many other psychic senses, this is a simplified categorization. Since there are so many others, using as few words as possible is beneficial. Most other perceptions come about through use of one or more of these six in combination.

Physical perceptions, the way we experience our material world, are so obvious that we are almost always *consciously* aware of them. Emotional responses, on the other hand, are sometimes so subtle that only searching deep in the subconscious can discover their origin. They can both be brought to *conscious* awareness. Psychic perceptions, however, come from a dimension with which we are usually unfamiliar. Under most circumstances, without knowing how to do it, they are impossible to pinpoint.

To demonstrate psychic perception functioning, take the case of "hunches." A "hunch" is a foreknowledge that something *is about to happen.* It may be in the context of guessing the outcome of some event, such as "That horse will win the second race." The *source* of that knowledge, how we could have foretold the future, as it were, is sometimes difficult for us to say. It could be simply a "lucky guess" or a random correctness. But some hunches are based in another dimension. The data comes through psychic perception, subliminal functioning that is beyond conscious awareness.

We are able to know something, have vast wisdom about it without conscious material knowledge, through direct contact with Universal Consciousness. Our non-physical sixth sense has the ability to gather an infinite amount of information through spiritual functioning in another dimension and influence our thought processes with it. Since all history, past, present, and future, coexists in Universal Consciousness, by making contact our psychic perceptions can identify future trends and cause its impression to affect thought. Hence, the superphysical source of some "hunches."

Psychic perceptions contact more than history on the highest level of pure essence. While there, it also receives information on which we base many of our *emotional* responses.

For example, say a woman is talking to a friend at a party. While the two are conversing, the woman senses someone standing behind her. She looks over her shoulder to see a nice looking, well-dressed man. He smiles, they exchange pleasantries and he leaves. The whole insignificant experience was far from pleasant to her for unknown reasons. The woman had a strange, inexplicable sense of foreboding in the man's presence.

First of all, the woman sensed someone behind her. There was no way her physical senses could have perceived the man's presence. There may even have been no change in air pressure that could signal such a thing. Her psychic perceptions had made contact with the man's psychic energy. She perceived the man's presence through other than her physical senses.

Next, all the while they talked, the woman had a strange unidentifiable feeling of apprehension. If her psychic perceptions had come into contact with *negative energy* in the man's psychic field, such a reaction would be expected. Another piece of important non-material information had made its effect known without use of the physical senses.

Psychic perception is sometimes described as "supernatural," being above and beyond the natural world. In fact, psychic senses are just as natural as the physical senses except that they deal in another dimension, or *another nature*. They are innately existing, spontaneous, unaffected receptors of the highest sphere of being.

Psychic perceptions are as accurate, sometimes more than their physical counterparts. If a non-appropriate emotional reaction results, it comes about through distortion, fallacious associations in the *second* sphere of being. Extrasensory, which is outside the scope of the physical, senses are exact and undistorted, as they are perceived. Emotional association or misinterpretation could confuse their meaning. Of themselves, they are precise.

In addition to receipt of incidental information, psychic perceptions include other phenomena. One of these perceptions is clairvoyance, which is "seeing" at a distance without *physical* connection. Telepathy is contact between psychic energies without *physical* connection. Other phenomenon are: precognition (a foreknowledge of future events); psychometry (the contact of the essence of a person by contacting the essence of an object belonging to the person); psychokinesis (manipulation of an object by use of psychic energy). There are innumerable other occurrences, many of which we experience daily.

Every person we meet and every object we pass has its own unique psychic energy field. Like a fingerprint, the energy in individual psychic fields is singular and identifiable. Some are generally positive, some are negative. Our psychic senses contact this energy and make it available for emotional use. Since some of this energy we contact constantly is unimportant to us, unless some emotional response should be called for, it will rarely, if ever, be noted. Whether we recognize it or not, psychic energy is all around us.

In the case of reception of highly charged energy, a conscious effect is sometimes noticed. We may "feel" the negativity inherent in some *place* or *person*, a generalized sensation of being ill at ease. Maybe we walk into an old abandoned house and, for unknown reasons, feel extremely uncomfortable around it. We can feel total well being, great calm in the presence of strong positivity. People, places, and things make contact between their psychic fields and ours, influencing all three spheres of being.

We get a wealth of healthy information that could aid our survival through our psychic perceptions. When we talk to someone, for example, whether stranger or friend, we make value judgments about them that are not based on physical awareness. We may feel that a particular person is "nice" although his/her appearance, mannerisms or speech show no outward sign of that fact. We might come into contact with someone who we know is supposed to be a pleasant, jolly person, but whom we feel uncomfortable around. For some reason, we get "bad vibes" from him/her. There is no other than a psychic basis for these perceptions. Our information is beyond the scope of physical sense.

With so much sensory information flooding our emotional sphere, an insufficient awareness of *which* of those perceptions has a purely psychic origin can cause a great deal of confusion and distress. If we are unaware of the highest form of perception, we cannot use it to its best advantage. We could avoid trying to be friendly to someone who our perceptions correctly tell us is having a negative influence on our spiritual sphere of being. By recognizing which psychic information is coming from contact with another person's psychic energy field, we just might find that our emotional response to them has been distorted. Their energy is actually positive though our emotional reaction was incorrectly negative. A recognition of the subtle influence psychic perception has upon the emotions would mean that we would have a deeper awareness of our omnipresent non-material environment.

When we have underdeveloped psychic senses or when we are unable to distinguish between psychic and physical sensations, a lot of sensory information is coming in of which we are not even subconsciously *aware*. Because our conscious awareness of psychic perception is minimal, the bulk of valuable extrasensory information goes unnoticed. But, if we are aware of it, the data could be used to form more appropriate emotional reactions.

Psychic perception is natural and healthy. Awareness of it is equally important and healthy. By developing them to their optimum capacity, we could receive or transmit more beneficial information and more precisely and accurately interpret them. Underdeveloped psychic perceptions and the awareness of them severely handicap *spontaneous emotional response.*

Insufficient psychic perception coupled with a lack of awareness of it, causes discomfort and distress in all three spheres of being.

<u>INEFFECTIVE COMMUNICATION</u>

This particular cause does not belong primarily to the spiritual sphere. Rather it is presented here because it is an omnipresent cause, a prevalent negative influence in all three. Since it is foremost of all causes, its discussion is properly an overview after the others.

The importance of communication in our lives cannot be overstated. It is that ability that permits us to talk to others and to help them understand how we feel about them, how we feel about ourselves and about our opinions of our environment. Through communication, we express and assert ourselves. In short, we interact positively *when we communicate.*

Communication is not simply *talking.* It involves others *understanding our thoughts, our feelings,* and not just *hearing* us. When we communicate, we *make ourselves understood* by allowing others to *get into us* fully.

The art of communication, like effective writing or public speaking, is an "art." It is not limited to making ourselves understood by others. It is also necessary for us to *understand them.*

When we cannot communicate *effectively,* we are unable to fully get into another person's problems. We cannot *identify* with them or understand them in context with our similarities.

A third part of effective communication deals with understanding *ourselves.* If we cannot communicate between our own internal spheres, troubles will constantly crop up which we fail to recognize because of a lack of *interaction* or understanding between them.

In years past, the phrase "communication gap" was coined to explain the inability of people to understand each other. Without effective communication, we cannot appreciate someone else's thoughts, ideas, concerns, hopes or their *reality.* We cannot get fully *into them.*

The art of communication does not imply that we need to *agree* with a differing opinion, thought or idea we consider unjustified. What it *does* mean, however, is that we *appreciate* someone's position, that we recognize their *being,* their freedom to express themselves as they deem appropriate. We need not agree with their opinions, but we must be able to *make our disagreement understood*, by others and by ourselves, and we have an obligation to *understand them*.

"Sympathy" in response to someone means basically that we feel similarly, that we feel sorry for his or her troubles. "Empathy," on the other hand, implies *identification*, that, agree or not, we understand their position and recognize and reinforce their right to effectively express themselves.

There are some people we come across in life who we consider "good talkers." "He certainly can express himself well!" "I can really *identify* with what she says," ad infinitum. These are our expressions of empathy with another person who has *communicated* himself/herself to us. Likewise, we can occasionally say the same thing about ourselves, such as "Boy, I sure made *that* point!"

Without enhanced communication, four separate, though identical, problems occur as a consequence. 1. We get along only *sporadically* with others. 2. We fail to *understand* others and ourselves. 3. We are frequently "misunderstood." 4. We do not have adequately *spontaneous* interactions, i.e. we tend to hear "what someone *means*" or what we *think* they mean, interpreting their statements rather than understanding and accepting their expressions.

We need to "say what we mean" as the old admonition goes, so that others will adequately understand us. If those we care about fail to recognize the full import of our words or our feelings, we cannot hope for a full relationship. Every being needs understanding and support from others. If we cannot *communicate* this need, we will rarely *receive a benefit*.

Similarly, we need to understand others, interact with them, and recognize their natural dignity and basic equality with us and to satisfy their needs, as well as our needs, of acceptance.

Communication is like a two way street. If we communicate effectively, others understand, empathize and recognize our worth as equals. The fulfillment of that need in us sparks communication on *their* part, fulfillment of *their* needs. Communication then enhances the well being of *each* party.

In the all-important word, the prefix "com-" indicates the Latin root, meaning "with." Communication is understanding, recognition, respect *between* people, *with* them, and not *by ourselves*. We communicate effectively, we *understand*, they communicate back with us. We *commu*nicate together.

Ineffective communication means that we will be frequently frustrated when others react to *what we mean* rather than the idea we *express*. We are again frustrated when we get something someone else didn't *mean*.

Communication is essentially accepting a person's expressions for what they are, expressions. We need to *accept* opinions *as opinions*, not gospel. That they are opinions rightfully expressed is indubitable. We need not *agree* with an opinion to accept it, understand it or *communicate* with the person making the expression.

A breakdown in communication results in many serious avoidable problems. From depression ("Nobody understands me!") to anger ("That's not what I meant."), to unhappiness ("Why did she <u>say</u> that. It hurt."), many other deleterious interpretations result from *ineffective communication.*

When our ability to interrelate is seriously compromised by a lack of *mutual understanding,* we cause distress within ourselves. If we do not express ourselves adequately or if we fail to empathize with another person's position, then we set up a chain of inappropriate reactions. In this way, ineffective communication causes serious distress in all three spheres of being.

ON THE CAUSES: A CONCLUSION

These ten causes of misery are by no means the *only* causes there are. For each individual there will probably be some unique *individual* causes. Those discussed represent the *major* causes of misery in each sphere of being: constriction of body freedom, poor health, unhealthy sexual inhibitions in the physical, phobias, unhealthy stereotypes, destructive love/hate, non-productive fantasy life in the emotional, and poor concentration/comprehension, insufficient psychic perception/awareness, and overshadowing and contributing to all the other causes, ineffective communication, discussed in the spiritual sphere section.

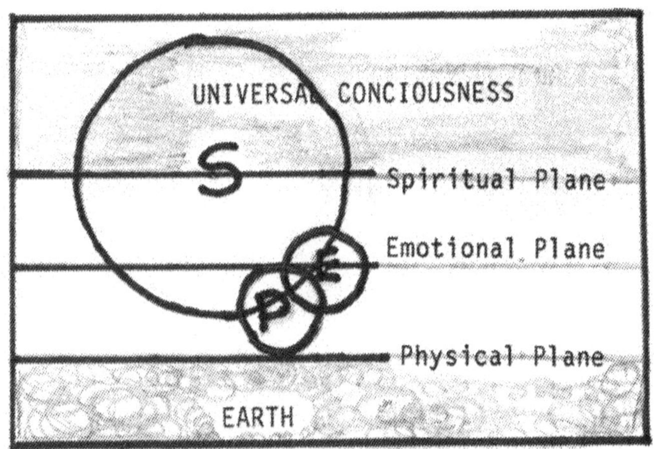

ILLUSTRATION 8

Because of their intimate interrelationship, the causes *directly involved* in each sphere adversely affect functioning in the other two. A cause in one sets up a malevolent effect in the others.

The cures to these causes are presented next in Part 2. Since they are so interconnected, *inter-causes* have *inter-cures*.

All of these causes are discussed for one prime reason: help with understanding and recognition of their full import will hopefully lead to

THE CONQUEST OF MISERY.

PART 2:

THE CURES TO MISERY

*Moderation is best, and
to avoid all extreme.*
—Plutarch

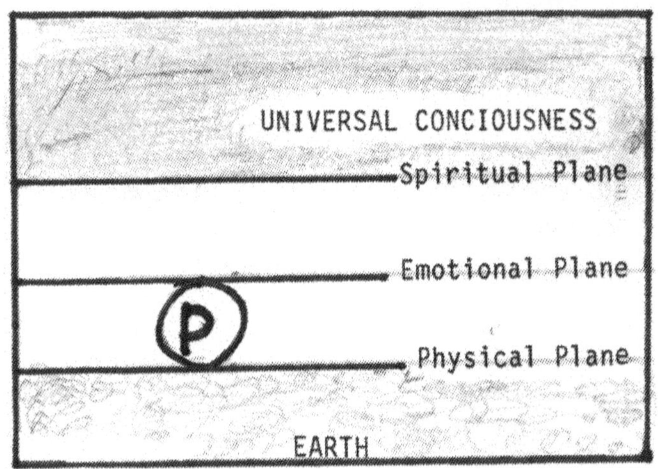

ILLUSTRATION 8

PHYSICAL CURES

The discussion in Part I centered on ten major causes of misery. Though they are not the *only* causes, they are perhaps the *most prevalent.* But important as they might be, their cures are not so simple.

There are many means to any end. Very few final goals have one, *and only one*, method of reaching them. The same is true of cures to misery. Even though a cause may call for a relatively simple cure, there are *many ways* of implementing it.

Generally, a variety of cures to the discussed major causes of misery are presented here. There are usually several methods presented for achieving the end result of any specific cure. Just as causes are sometimes complex in origin, so too, their related cures are varied.

BODY FREEDOM

Since it is apparent that constriction of body freedom causes varying degrees of misery, the obvious solution to the distressful condition is to remove the constriction. The cure *is* to increase body freedom, but *how* to achieve that goal can take several directions.

First, the simplest way to get rid of all constriction of body movement is to take off the clothes. By removing the *cause* of constriction, the unhealthy effects disappear. Without clothing, our bodies have more than a freedom of movement or a lack of irritating signals being sent to the brain. Another major advantage of going *au naturel* is that all of our physical senses are able to communicate directly with our environment. Our skin can breathe freely through its pores without the block of clothing. We can touch the grass with our whole body, feel the cool air and sunshine that is diminished or completely stopped by clothes. We can better relate to our world, appreciate it better, and respond to it more fully.

Gymnosophy embodies the philosophy behind social nudism, casting off chains of slavery to stereotypes, prejudices, even nervousness and inhibitions by removing the clothes. When nude, our whole attitude toward our self-image improves. The way we see others and inter-relate with them improves dramatically. Clothing is sometimes a barrier to spontaneous expression.

The concept of gaining more emotional, spiritual, and physical freedom takes nudity to a more complex sociological level as a cure to distress. Gymnosophy has a definite, secure place as a viable method for alleviating distress.

Gymnosophy as a routine cure to misery can be accomplished in two ways. The first is to live in a nudist environment, a retreat where only people who believe in gymnosophy live; people who accept the nudity of others as a matter of healthy fact. The second is to practice gymnosophy in the privacy of our home.

Our freedom to practice this cure to misery is modified *in practice*. The simple fact that if we exercise our belief in nudism *in public*, and involve people who *do not share* our attitude about the beneficial effects of nudity, we put ourselves in a situation that seriously compromises our survival. If we walk down a public street flagrantly violating the deeply rooted social sanction against appearing nude in public, someone could very well complain about our "indecency" due to stereotype-controlled reactions. We leave ourselves open to be arrested, or at least lectured, on social responsibility. Whether arrest and/or punishment for nudity is reasonable or not, others have a right *not to participate* in our activities.

The ideal would be for all people to encourage individual freedom in others, to share the view that *if we do not violate another person's freedom*, we have a right to do what we please. The fact is that we *do not* live in an ideal world. By virtue of living with people who have very divergent views, our *absolute* freedom must be compromised *in practice*. Our *right to exercise* our freedom must be modified when in the world of those who would deny us that freedom. ("When in Rome...")

The word "public" defines an area where our freedom must be compromised. It denotes a place where there is no *agreement* on accepting our choices, where social sanctions are rarely in favor of relaxed individual freedom. "Private", on the other hand, designates a place where there is an agreement to accept the same conduct. It doesn't mean that we have to practice our beliefs alone—privately. If we prefer, we can practice our beliefs in a group setting with others that share our desires to practice this particular freedom.

When in private, our freedom of choice is protected by our surroundings. In public, the rights of others are of foremost importance. In private, the observer knows what he's going to see and does not object to it. In effect, his freedom becomes irrelevant. If our private activities offend someone, they can leave, but we should not be punished.

Besides getting rid of the constriction caused by clothing altogether, we can lessen the distress when we have no alternative but to wear clothes in public. The more rough the texture of the cloth, the more irritation to tender nerve endings on the skin. A tough cloth causes more negative sensations to the brain than does smoother textured fabric. By wearing soft cloth, our bodies will at least not be scraped by a rough, irritating surface. Even with smooth, pliable fabric our nerve endings will be sending negative impulses. At least the message will be *less negative*.

A third way of achieving more freedom is to wear clothes that do not restrict free movement. Loose clothing aids in allowing easier muscle movement. Tight fitting clothes, if designed to fit our anatomy and made of stretchable fabric, allow for about the *same amount* of freedom as loose dress. Tight fitting clothes may not *appear* to be an alternative, but they can allow for the same comfort.

A final method of lessening the *effects* of constriction, or *increasing the benefit* of wearing clothes, to be more positive, is by increasing our self-esteem *because* of it. If we wear clothing as an extension of our personalities or as an expression of how we feel about ourselves, in short, dressing as we change our moods, we can stay within the *practical* social sanctions while enhancing our well being at the same time.

It is true that gymnosophy offers the only *total* cure to the misery caused by the constriction of body freedom due to clothing. In our day-to-day *public* existence, getting rid of even some clothing *irritation* offers a successful partial cure. Although *absolute* would be preferable, *partial* is satisfactory.

As with other concepts, cures offer happiness in proportion to their effectiveness. Eliminating all of the distress brings *maximum* well being. Erasing *part* of it gives less. Because of the inter-connection of the three spheres of being, even *lessening* distress increases *overall* well being. A partial cure to the misery caused by constriction of body freedom brings us that much closer to healthy equilibrium.

Because the constriction of clothing can cause so much distress in the lower, physical sphere of being, body freedom also has an effect in the higher sphere of being. Body freedom creates emotional and, hence, spiritual well being.

INCREASED VITALITY

Good health involves more than simply not being ill, not having many aches and pains, and not being distressed. Optimum physical condition demands *vitality*. Vitality is the by-product of good health. The two are inseparable.

The concept of vitality, in one of its broader definitions, concerns "the continuation of life or full physical vigor." It includes other concepts, such as "vim". Similar to vigor and a part of vitality, all three words describe the *dynamic power* of the healthy body.

There seems to be little debate that physical vitality is concomitant with good health. But there is debate over just how to achieve it. If we analyze the simpler ideas first, the more complex arguments may become easier to understand.

Exercise is certainly an important part of achieving vitality. By making the body's gross structure strong, we receive such diverse benefits as slowing the aging process, increasing mobility, having graceful movement, and ensuring healthy internal organs. It can also help to prevent serious illness and disease. The benefits are universally accepted, but the preferred *methods of obtaining them* differ.

On the one hand is the concept of "body building" or lifting weights. The idea also includes other remedies for bringing about an improved body, and the part that deals with exercise is most *apropos* here. This school of thought holds that development of the muscles into strong, powerful tools increases vitality. Physical strength is equated with a sound, healthy body. As in most well-meaning theories, actual practice can reveal fallacies in the idea. Bodybuilding is not unique in having its drawbacks. Most other regimens share the same traits.

Another procedure that deals with the *entire being* rather than just *muscular* development has been around for many years. Yoga, as a philosophy, has had remarkable success in both achieving increased vitality and in the staying power as a force. Yogic theory has been incorporated into many of the world's older major religions and philosophies, as well as being the basis for numerous newer churches.

The basic theory of *hatha yoga*, which is *physical* development, revolves around the Eastern view of life. Yin/yang implies the central theme that by opposition muscles can be strengthened. Exercise in the yogic tradition is very different from Western methods. The oldest regimen of non-strenuous body movement, "exercises" through postures called *"asanas,"* achieves the goal of optimum muscle *tone* instead of *strength*. Yoga exercise leads to increased vitality while being relaxing, and at the same time strengthening coordination, vigor and reducing aches and pains.

Each of the two schools of exercise methods probably has some erroneous theories, and neither is best for *everyone*. Through rigorous practice, it is generally agreed that yoga has fewer physical drawbacks.

The primary reason yoga is often singled-out as the most beneficial of the philosophies is that it involves a *total* approach to health. Besides having effective methods for improving the *physical* part of man, yoga also increases emotional and spiritual vitality through other procedures for exercising the higher sphere.

In the yoga method, the important task of physical hygiene is achieved through the literal cleansing of the orifices of the body. There is a very specific ritualized regimen for keeping all of the body's openings to the external world pure. The ears, nostrils, mouth, vagina, the penile opening, and anus are kept free of disease with this regimen. Problems can be checked before they can infect the interior of the body.

Brushing our teeth, bathing, *taking care of our bodies* is also a major impetus of the yoga tradition, a beneficial adjunct to any method of achieving vitality. Cleanliness of body is a powerful asset to getting and maintaining good health.

Next comes the necessity of proper diet for optimum physical well being. Our bodies need food to function. We require energy to discharge our physical, emotional, and spiritual duties. The more efficient the foods, the better we function. It follows that the *quality* of what we eat affects the *quality* of our performance.

It is generally accepted that excessive amounts of additives and chemicals are in what we commonly call "junk food". While certain natural plants are considered downright unhealthy, there are varying opinions about what is best. There would seem to be no consensus on which foods are healthy and life enhancing, even though there is a general idea of what is worst.

The crux of the problem is the biological fact that man is *omnivorous*. We can eat just about anything, while most other animals eat certain types of food exclusively, usually meat or vegetation. Man is both *carnivorous* (meat eating) and/or herbivorous (vegetation eating), which means he is *omni*vorous. The ongoing debate over which food is *most healthy* revolves around this equivocation of man's desires.

The school of thought of vegetarianism holds that vegetables are inherently *more healthy* than "contaminating" meat. Meat-eaters, on the other hand, defend their bias toward an *overabundance of meat* in the daily diet. The optimum dietary efficiency probably lies somewhere *between* the two poles, though opinions vary widely even among so-called "experts".

A balanced diet including *some* meat and *some* vegetables with representatives of all food groups is certainly *not unhealthy*. Each kind of food has its own attributes. Some "natural" foods can be less than health-productive. Some, in fact, are *un*healthy. While some man-made chemistry can *aid* our well being, *too much* meat, or *vegetables* for that matter, can cause adverse reactions in our body against certain constituents of their various foods.

It might seem odd that many people in *both* schools appear equally healthy, testimonials to their correctness. Because man is an *adaptable* animal, and because we can adjust to almost any condition, even our eating habits can be reconciled with our desires. If we *want* to eat only meat or *only* vegetables, we can enjoy doing it and stay healthy. A *balanced* diet improves this ability. We adapt *more easily* to a *variety* of foods and increase vitality in the process.

Physical disease has perhaps more to do with our optimum health than any other area. How we feel determines our success at living. That much is universally agreed. It would seem much more difficult to agree on *how* to eradicate disease from the human condition.

"Medical science" is ordinarily defined in *practical terms* as a body of knowledge about physical functions, combined with methods, for preventing and/or curing disease. Objective diagnosis is the process of determining a cause-and-effect relationship between disease and the body through *physical* examination. Physical manipulations of the body such as objective diagnosis, inoculations, and surgery are methods of controlling human ailments. The *practice* of medicine, as opposed to the *theory*, is more often referred to as an "art" rather than a "science". The requisite skill inherent in one human being trying to analyze another's internal problems depends many times on the physician's *subjective judgement* of the objective facts.

Another means of disease control involves the highest sphere of being. Occult tradition holds that disease of the body is a direct *effect* of spiritual distress. By concentrating upon determining *spiritual* causes of disease, *spiritual* healing intends to find the cure by restoring and/or enhancing *physical* health.

Both methods of curing physical ills have their place in the control and eradication of disease. They each have affected cures considered "impossible" or "miraculous". Medical science has cured some extremely serious diseases that spiritual methods have not. Spiritual cures have prevailed occasionally over medical science. They *each* have intrinsic value.

A *balance* of methods of conquering disease would perhaps be most efficient toward the end goal of increasing vitality. Some problems can be stopped through spiritual means while others are better handled with physical medical science. If one fails to produce a solution, the other may be able. Medical and spiritual healing can have *equal* merit in many instances. Instead of being alternatives, *together* they create a viable method for achieving good health.

A third area of disease control concerns itself with the second sphere of being. *Psychosomatic medicine* holds that many diseases have an *emotional cause.* By solving second sphere distress, the disease often disappears. Holistic medicine also views disease as more than only a *physical* phenomenon. Poor health, they say, has its roots in both first and second spheres.

While their individual focus of attention is on different areas of the being, each method of controlling disease has its unique contribution for the cure of physical misery. In *combination*, instead of *exclusively*, they offer tremendous possibilities for increasing vitality.

In discussing health, the subject of habits becomes important. While we generally think of a "habit" as an unconscious action we *always take* in reaction to a similar stimulus, it can include *more* than that. The broad term "habit" is often applied to most of our *pursuits of pleasure*.

Tobacco, alcohol, drugs and many other pastimes are called "habits" simply for wont of another name. That they actually *are* pursuits of pleasure follows from their physical/psychological *effects* of making us feel better, "high" to varying degrees.

The use of drugs plays a very important role in most of our lives whether they are for simple aches and pains or for getting loaded. *Anything* we ingest which alters body chemistry can be classified as a "drug." Some drugs, like insulin, are mentally inactive. We feel no psychological effects. Other drugs, like cocaine, LSD, marijuana, and many more have strong psychic effects on us. These effects are generally pleasurable, with heightened sensory awareness and altered states of consciousness. These *drugs of pleasure* can pose a much more serious threat to health than disease if they are *abused*.

Since some drugs are illegal, their use could cause *legal* complications. This is certainly a concern for using drugs because a person might get into trouble for using them. Legal or not, most psychoactive drugs have strong side effects. They range from drowsiness to hallucinations, sometimes even to death, if the dosage is too massive. If used in moderation, it would seem to be a matter of debate whether *lasting* side effects will manifest. Abuse of any drug, even such common chemistry as aspirin or sleeping pills, can have long-term debilitating effects. Since drugs put chemicals into our body that are not normally there, *excessive use* or *uncontrolled intake* causes serious health problems.

Psychoactive drug use, as an aid to relieving physical distress, seems to be a healthy alternative practice. Recreational drug use, if done for a healthy reason and not abused, is part of an important cure to physical misery and aids in the pursuit of vitality.

Moderation in all things, not as in Prohibition, is no more than common sense. *Besides* making good sense, there are certain basic facts that make moderation a logical alternative to excessive use:

1. By not going to extremes in anything we do, we can ameliorate potential problems concomitant with receiving *maximum* benefit.
2. By being able to recognize the warning signs of malfunction, we can treat excesses with moderation and, in the physical sphere, stave off serious problems by taking care of the *minor* ills.

3. By allowing ourselves to change our opinions and moderate our thoughts, we can ensure that we will eventually find the cure that best suits our needs in the higher spheres.

Vitality is the by-product of a healthy body, the reward for success in physical enhancement. Through our attainment of vigor and robust health, we gain a cure to a large amount of physical misery and positively affect the other two spheres of being. Vitality helps to create contentment.

<u>HEALTHY SEXUAL EXPRESSION</u>

Our sexual instincts are directed toward basic survival, and thus, are a powerful force within us. Frustration of that instinctual power causes severe distress.

The inhibition of healthy sexual expression comes about in many ways, as discussed earlier. In presenting methods of, and reasons *for*, cures to the distressful condition, a further analysis is necessary.

Although the subject of stereotypes will be more fully discussed under "Emotional Cures," there are certain stereotypical/phobic reactions that directly concern sexual expression.

"A man *should* feel sexually aroused *all the time*." "A woman *should*, or *should not*, achieve orgasm," "A man *should not* concern himself with his partner's pleasure." These are only a few of the many irrational demands that wreak untold distress on most people. A person doesn't *have* to do anything, feel any *particular way*, worry, fret or concern him/herself with doing or not doing stereotyped behavior.

It is *not necessary* for our partners and us to achieve multiple or spontaneous orgasm. "Performance anxiety," nervousness and general emotional distress, presents itself because of an irrational *need* to perform. This is a socially conditioned *demand* that we *must* be sexually aroused when called upon and further *enjoy* sexual relations *no matter what*. For one reason or another, there are times when a man cannot achieve an erection. Premature ejaculation can happen occasionally to an otherwise "normal" man. Many things that interfere with a satisfying sexual expression are natural and not *actually* unhealthy unless the problem *becomes chronic*.

One thing we need to realize is that sex is to be *enjoyed*. When and how we wish to express ourselves is our choice. We have *no obligation* to perform in any particular way. The most important factor in our sexual expression is our *enjoyment of* it.

Spontaneity is likewise important. The ability to enjoy without premeditated thought or deliberation ensures *naturalness*. If we must think, plan, or compute before we can enjoy ourselves, we are no longer *genuine*. Our expression is being controlled by external considerations, phobias, stereotypes or other unhealthy emotions, and become *artificial behavior*. When we can react as the mood strikes, without excessive deliberation, we are acting *naturally*, as we *feel*, not as we *think*.

Another condition we need to consider in curing sexual inhibition is *guilt*. We are *conditioned* to feel distress when we perform an *"immoral"* act. More often than not, the guilt is *misplaced*.

Each of us has a *conscience* that makes judgements about right and wrong. It bases its conclusions upon memory experience, consequences and "moral senses," our conception of "good and bad." When we either perform, or even *think about performing*, an act we have been conditioned to believe "immoral," conscience reacts with guilt.

Guilt is sometimes justified, natural and healthy. If we propose to act in an *unhealthy* way, which *also may be* "immoral," guilt stops us by creating distress *before the fact*. Guilt is a deterrent to unhealthy behavior.

Guilt also makes its presence known, however, even when it is misplaced. We are conditioned to believe, for instance, that nonperformance, as an inability to *successfully* perform sexually (a stereotyped expectation) is "bad." In response we feel guilt. Sometimes it is misplaced. It causes distress, though not in reaction to a *natural* situation, one which is not unhealthy. If a being cannot perform sexually, it is not even a *serious problem* necessarily, much less being unhealthy. Often times, *misplaced* guilt creates unnecessary misery.

While some sexual expression stereotypes are unhealthy and lead to frustration of healthy expression, others are life enhancing. Like *justified* guilt, the moral dictate against rape, for example, is in response to a life-threatening, violent act against another with intent to rob him/her of *basic freedom*. Not only rape, but also many other sexual expression stereotypes are healthy and enhance well being as well as group well being.

Sex out of wedlock (before/after/during marriage), sex with a partner of the same gender, and masturbation are just some of the healthy sexual expressions we are denied because of *unhealthy* moral dictates. By expressing our sexuality in those and other ways and using our freedom of choice responsibly, we ensure our enhanced well being.

The variety of ways to express our sexuality is virtually unlimited. We engage in group sex, orgies, masturbation, anal and oral sex, and men/women having sex with their own gender. Without guilt, we can even enjoy recreational sex without love, just because it is healthy and life affirming. In the alternative, we can decide to *not express* our sexuality at all, or to be asexual. Homosexuality and bisexuality are also alternatives to heterosexuality.

There are not as many methods of *implementing* the cure, but there are several means to the end of getting rid of unhealthy sexual inhibitions. First, we can discuss our sexuality and related feelings, such as guilt, stereotypes and more, with someone else. We can discuss the topic with *several* others in a *collective* investigation. We can even *"let ourselves go"* with or without aphrodisiacs and do whatever we *feel*. We can express our sexuality, or not, without inhibitions and without need of assistance. There are many effective ways to get rid of unhealthy sexual inhibitions.

Any discussion of sexual matters necessarily includes the subject of *responsibility*. Children are the product of heterosexual intercourse. A woman will not *necessarily* become pregnant by the sex act, but it *is* a real and present possibility. With so many unwanted children in the world already, we have an obligation to ourselves, to humanity, *and the unborn child*, not to bring any more into the world. A child has enough problems growing up without the added burden of being unwanted and having to endure the emotional and physical hardships he/she will meet. With the use of either a condom or sexual abstinence, sexual tension can be eliminated.

Euphemistically known as "children of love," they are more accurately "children of irresponsibility." Unwanted pregnancies *can* be prevented in many ways. Some ways are with intelligent and effective birth control, alternative sexual expression, common sense, and knowledge of our bodies. An unwanted pregnancy can also be terminated before an unwanted child is born, *before it's too late*. We each have a responsibility to prevent unwanted and unloved life.

In deciding whether a certain expression is healthy for us, there are a few prerequisites that can make the choice easier.

1. Is the expression going to be pro-survival for our partner(s) and us? Will it probably *benefit* each of us and enhance our well being?
2. Is our expression uninhibited and based entirely on positive consideration instead of negative influences?
3. Is our expression *spontaneous* and natural?
4. Does our partner consent to be involved in our expression? Is he/she willing?
5. Finally, are we or are we *not* being controlled by misplaced guilt?

If the answer to each of the above questions is an unqualified "yes," the expression is healthy. If any one of the answers is "no," the chosen sexual expression is *un*healthy. It is just that simple to determine the merits of our proposed behavior.

The admonition, "If it feels good, do it!" says volumes about sexual inhibitions. Very few taboos are reasonable when the *effect* of the frustration makes it *not* feel good. However, just because "it feels good" doesn't automatically make it *healthy*. Orgasm is accompanied by pleasure no matter if the *reason* for the expression is *unhealthy*. A more life enhancing admonition would be "If it feels good, do it *unless it is also unhealthy!*"

Sex is without doubt one of the most rewarding, joyous, mystical and ecstatic encounters we can have. The gratification of our most basic and pervasive instinct takes us to new levels of awareness and understanding, besides being *physically healthy*.

By healthy expression of our sexuality without inhibitions and without the counter-productive influence of phobias, stereotypes and other unhealthy, distorting emotions, we enhance our physical well being. Because of their intimate interrelationship, we also achieve enhanced *emotional* contentment and spiritual growth.

> **It is extraordinary how emotional**
> **storms one may weather in safety if**
> **one is ballast with ever so little gold.**
> **—William McFee**

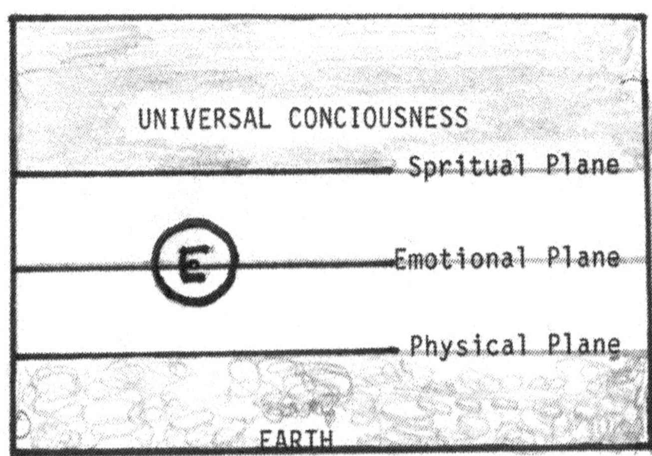

ILLUSTRATION 9

EMOTIONAL CURES

ELIMINATION OF PHOBIC REACTIONS

Before beginning our discussion of how to get rid of phobic reactions, we need to clarify an important point. A phobia is an *irrational* fear reaction based upon a misinterpretation of the facts, while *fear* itself is an instinctual reaction against a stimulus that *actually* threatens our survival. Fear is natural, healthy and life enhancing. Phobic reactions are unhealthy and self-destructive.

Fears are necessary to our continued success in life because they force us to act against things that *seriously threaten* our survival. By being against them, fears are *pro-survival*. Phobias, on the other hand, are reactions to an *imagined* threat, a threat to our survival that has been distorted and may not be *real*. This distinction will help greatly when discussing methods of cure.

Since phobias are a product of emotional distortion, the only way to conquer them is to delve into the subconscious and examine exactly how they developed. We are able to overcome phobic reactions by recognizing them as such. Once we fully understand where the phobia came from, how and why it developed and its irrationality, we no longer have to react to its distortion. If we recognize that it is a phobic reaction, we needn't allow its expression again.

Investigating the subconscious is not quite as simple as it might seem. It is called *sub*conscious because it exists *below awareness*. We cannot look into it by ordinary thinking since, under most circumstances, we would not be *aware* of subconscious information if we *happened to contact it*. We do need another method to accomplish the objective.

One way of looking *below consciousness* is through deep introspection. By training the mind to raise subconscious thought *up to our awareness*, we are able to understand our deeper store of memories. Reverie is one way of allowing subconscious information to surface where we can examine it *consciously*, using logic and reason to analyze it.

Yoga provides a means for getting down into the subconscious and bringing memory up to awareness. Through extensive relaxation and controlled breathing, it is possible to *still the mind*, to get it into a state of non-action. When the mind is completely relaxed, it becomes easier to reach subconscious memory. In a state of calm, bringing information to consciousness is as simple as *allowing it to surface*.

Once memories are in our consciousness, we can start to examine them. We can easily determine *which* information is related to *what*. The associations make themselves known through our reactions to each memory. They trigger other memories that demonstrate an obvious connection. We can see where they became connected and why. With that recognition, the connections cease to be important as far as our future actions are concerned. After understanding them, the *influences* of irrational associations disappear. Phobic reactions are *effectively eliminated.*

Introspection is sometimes difficult because stilling the mind is very often extremely trying. Even so, with training and a *real desire to do it*, we can reach our subconscious by ourselves. Even if we do reach our subconscious mind in this manner, we can run into possible problems.

Associations are tricky things. When brought up to consciousness, irrational connections sometimes seem *logical*. It is as if some associations don't want us to *know about them*. They can sometimes fool us into believing they are rightly connected to something *they aren't*. These relationships are usually the result of severe trauma and are a powerful *defense* to a survival threat, *real or not*. Inasmuch as they are so strong, it is often the case that they are illusive to identify because they *appear* correct. We may not fully recognize an irrational association when we see it simply because of the powerful forces that bind associations together.

Those relationships we don't fully discover are generally the *most important*. They comprise the memories that are involved in most *serious* reactions. If we have correctly identified the source of a phobia, the reaction ceases to be controlling. But if we respond to phobic influence after our investigation, we have not recognized the *proper* source. If irrational associations are still controlling us, we have missed the correct relationship.

Solving this difficulty is possible, though time consuming and often frustrating. A faster, albeit less personal, method of discovering subconscious associations is through *group investigation.*

A "group" need not consist of more than two people talking and helping each other recognize associations. It is very often true that someone else can see flaws in our thinking when they seem logical *to us*. We are sometimes *too close* to the problem, and our vision becomes myopic. We can't see the *whole picture.* Many times other people can view our memories more objectively because they can see the issue more clearly than we can. They are able to see a much broader area since they are *further from the problem.* Through communication we allow ourselves to be honest in our discussion of important memory as it comes up. We recognize associations of which we might otherwise be unaware.

The same principle lies behind "group therapy." The process has some negative associations in many people's minds. Images of insanity and mental patients desperately in need of psychiatric help may influence an inaccurate conception. It is certainly true that severe emotional disturbances most often require a group of *more than two* for a *variety* of possible reasons. The reason group therapy has a high rate of success is that associations that cause the most serious reactions are the most difficult to recognize. A group offers more points of view and more observations to increase the possibility of correct analysis. Because of the stigma attached to "group therapy," *collective awareness development* may be a better name for the process.

The reason others can see our problems *more clearly* is demonstrated in the old tale of the three handicapped men investigating the same animal. One blind man walked up to an elephant and felt its legs. To him the animal was obviously shaped like a tree trunk. The second blind man felt the elephant's tail and decided it was a rope. The third man felt the trunk and came to a visualization of a hose.

All three blind men were *partially* correct. The parts they touched *did* have the shapes they believed, but none of them could describe the *whole elephant.* Their blindness limited their investigation. A sighted observer looking from a distance could see the *total* animal and describe all its *parts* in context with the *whole* body. Besides being physically blind, each man was too close to the elephant to see it objectively. An outside observer, however, isn't so close as to be misled by *fragments.* The *entire picture* will be more accurate. For this reason, collective awareness development allows independent observers to view our attitudes objectively. Their distance from the subject allows them to "see" *more.*

Whether done through individual or group effort, both processes can lead to increased awareness and, consequently, the end of irrational, unhealthy associations. No matter how we do it, recognizing associations, being able to understand their origin and functions, diminishes their power over us.

Through introspection and awareness development, we can effectively eliminate phobic reactions and stop a great deal of serious emotional distress. The restoration of emotional equilibrium makes its life enhancing effects felt in the highest spheres of being.

<u>REDUCTION OF STEREOTYPES</u>

Similar to the way phobias are created, stereotypes also have associations at their root. However, stereotypes do not come about in response to a survival question. Instead, they are the products of *conditioning*.

Recognizing a stereotype is not as difficult as the process needed for discovering phobic associations. In this case, all that is basically necessary is to recognize an unhealthy stereotype when it *appears* and simply *stop being influenced by it*.

Again, the distinction between *healthy* and *unhealthy* stereotypes needs to be drawn. *Healthy stereotypes* are associations that tend to *enhance* our well being, improve our interrelationships with others. If it tends to be *destructive to* our well being or if it adversely influences our social interactions by creating a distorted response, the stereotype is unhealthy.

It was discussed earlier, but repetition here is important to understanding the process of recognition. A stereotype usually has the same basic structure, though particular wording or mental imagery may be different. "All __________ are/aren't __________." "Every __________ is/isn't __________." " __________ should/shouldn't __________." Stereotypes deal in all kinds of *absolutes* that are *always* true. They are generalizations about the future based on faulty associations to the past.

"All *animals are stupid*," "Every *minister is nice*," "*Men* shouldn't *cry*," are examples of fallacious stereotypes. All animals are *not* stupid. Some are highly intelligent. The generalization is fallacious on its face. *Not every* minister is nice. Some are miserable people, no doubt. Often it is true that men should cry, but there are occasions when crying would not be the *best* response. While most things are true sometimes, there are very few *absolutes* when dealing with people.

Interpretation of stereotypical commands is helpful in separating positive from destructive. That all animals are stupid is neither a logical nor *healthy* generalization. It distorts our objectivity by putting an *entire class* of creatures into one erroneous category. The reverse is also true, though less so. That all animals are intelligent is a matter of opinion, depending on the exact definition of "intelligent."

As in any other matter dealing with human behavior, stereotypes are primarily fallacious because they prevent *individual* reactions based on *specific* circumstances. Unhealthy stereotypes set up expectations based on *group* rather than individual determinations. Human responses and attitudes usually fall somewhere *between* the possible extremes, in *yin/yang* or not in either *yin or yang*.

Spontaneous expression under most circumstances is enhancing to our emotional equilibrium. It creates a non-forced reaction because it is not based on preconceptions. By setting up expectations through associations and conditioning, stereotypes rob us of our ability to react spontaneously. Instead, we use *deliberation*, planning our response in advance.

The *healthy* stereotype follows the same general rules. It deals in absolutes too, but is directed *toward* our well being instead of *against* it. "A *man* should *be responsible*." It is true most all the time and improves our self-image when we perform the stereotyped behavior. Such a stereotype is healthy *and beneficial*.

Awareness of stereotypes comes from recognizing them and limiting their influence over our reactions. By being aware of when a stereotypical association causes distortion, we can *ignore* its attempted control.

Again, the method of recognition is basically the same. Through introspection and observing our reactions to others or ourselves, we can decide whether a stereotype is *forcing* our interpretation of the facts. And, as before, this introspection can be achieved in several ways.

One method of bringing stereotypes to conscious awareness is simply to interpret associations as they come up. When a stereotypical response presents itself, we can recognize it as such and deal with it as necessary—*at the time*. It is most difficult at times to recognize a deeply conditioned association.

Another regimen that is *more* efficient is to discover stereotypical associations *before* confrontation and before the responses are actually *called for*. This introspection is simplified by calming the mind and allowing associations to make their presence known. As Max Heindel, author of many mystical treatises, put it so succinctly: "As we may see ourselves in the silvery surface of a lake on a calm day, so also the spirit most readily mirrors itself in the personality when we are serene and unruffled. When we still the mind, we can easily see what lies just beneath consciousness."

Stilling the mind can be accomplished in any way that we may find convenient. By doing it ourselves, once again, Yoga offers an efficient method. The same means of discovery used for determining those connected with phobias can help us recognize *stereotypical* associations. The end result is the same for both investigations. We recognize subconscious memory associations for what they really are!

A third way of achieving introspection is through group process. While collective awareness development works on a relatively deep level, delving into subconscious associations which may or may *not* be apparent, a parallel regimen looks at how we *act*, our observable behavior, to make the determination. By seeing our interactions and how we verbalize, think and relate to others, many times our responses to stereotypes become obvious.

Transactional Analysis is the name of one school of thought concerning how to conduct collective discovery. This concept revolves around the idea that there are three parts of a personality: Parent, Adult and Child. Each part concerns different areas of our associations. Parent is the authoritarian influence. Stereotypes, phobias, *conditioned reactions* that we've learned through being "told" they are so, as it were. Adult deals with reasoning, logical thinking and analysis. The Child section of our compartmentalized personality, in this view, is seen as the basis of our *spontaneous reactions*, our instinctive responses *without influence* of either Parent or Adult.

By recognizing the contamination that sometimes happens, and allowing each part of the personality to react without negative influences from the others, our responses slowly become more spontaneous.

It will be noted that although the words are different, the same *basic concepts* are involved in Parent (Emotional), Adult (Spiritual) and Child (Physical). Of course, the broad definitions are noticeably different, but the basic concepts behind them, the reasoning of the process of disturbance, are identical. In fact, in many other types of philosophies, similarities will occur.

While Transactional Analysis is only one of many schools that concern themselves with methods of achieving deep introspection, they achieve the same goal in the same way. Through collective analysis of our *observable behavior*, errors in the thinking, and irrational reactions become very apparent. It is this "gestalt" *(overall picture)* process of seeing the being as a *totality* and watching our interactions *objectively* that allows others to recognize our fallacious associations.

During introspection, even casually thinking of the stereotypes we come across every day, we will find a few, and perhaps many, that are, in fact, *healthy*. By analyzing them in context with our *enhanced well being*, the healthy ones become quite distinct from those that *damage* our equilibrium. These healthy stereotypes have beneficial effects upon our emotional responses and so can be separated from the *destructive ideations*, and thus nurtured. We can make healthy stereotypes *healthier* by recognizing them and incorporating them into our awareness.

The method is really unimportant. What is imperative is that we do recognize unhealthy stereotypical associations and not allow them reign over our reactions.

Whether through individual introspection or collective analysis, the process of recognizing stereotypical associations is essential to recapturing our spontaneity. By getting rid of destructive, unhealthy stereotypes and at the same time nurturing and intensifying healthy life enhancing associations, we restore emotional well being. This emotional improvement is felt on all levels.

<u>CONSTRUCTIVE LOVE/HATE</u>

The need for healthy emotional expression is the same for all of our reactions. By eliminating distortion caused by our associations, we are able to interrelate spontaneously, and thereby regain a natural, *unaffected* response.

Conditioning is the process that leads to destructive love/hate. We are taught ceaselessly from childhood that there are certain people in our lives who we have an *obligation* to love—no matter what! Whether they treat us badly, whether they hamper our happiness, we are still *required* to love them. Some parents actually imperil their child's survival. While *relatively* few parents inflict *physical* harm on their offspring, too many cause *emotional* damage. The distress these children often feel isn't obvious, but it is *real* and requires proper response.

It would again seem necessary to clarify distinctions at this point in our discussion. The word "love" signifies a myriad of emotions from "pure love" to plain "like," or a *preference* toward. "Hate", similarly, is not only maximum intensity against something, but it includes "dislike" or slight negativity. This distinction is important to keep in mind. When "hate" is called for, the appropriate emotion could be as innocuous as mild "dislike" and not necessarily the emotional intensity of the maximum expression against. Love/hate intensity must be kept in perspective and in context with the *amount* and *degree* of appropriate response.

If we *try* to *feel* love when a more appropriate response would be hate, our reaction becomes distorted, usually by fallacious stereotypes of how and why toward whom we *should* feel. How we *should react* may not be how we *actually* *feel*. When that is the case, our response is affected and untrue to ourselves. *It is unhealthy.*

Stereotypes that condition our ideas of what love/hate *should* be, how we *should* express it are deep-seated and powerful. They start in response to real survival stimuli. We *should* feel love for people who aid our well being. We *should* hate those who we feel imperil it. Stereotypical demands are very simple to follow, though often times *destructive*.

A balance of emotions would be at an optimum even when dealing with our own emotions. Very little calls for *pure love* as a response. Conversely, it is difficult to conceive of such a negative situation as would require *absolute hate*.

At any single moment, our responses will probably be degrees of *both* emotions simultaneously.

Recognizing whether the love/hate is appropriate and whether it is in proportion to the stimulus or contrary to it can eliminate destructive love/hate. When our expression reflects how we think, how we *should* respond rather than how we *feel*, our *affected reaction is unhealthy*.

Recognizing love/hate is simple because our emotional world responds very strongly to it. If we feel strong familial love, we receive a warm, pleasurable feeling, a sense of joy as a consequence. Hate, on the other hand, makes us feel anxious, nervous, cold, devoid of happiness, and miserable. Being aware of whether the feeling is *either* love *or* hate (or love/hate) is generally facile.

Since love/hate strikes so deeply at our survival, recognizing *distorted responses* is difficult. The easiest, although perhaps not the most efficient, method of discovering their appropriateness is to *get in touch* with our feelings and become *fully aware* of how our responses *affect us*, how they influence our lives, and how they *make us feel*. If we feel happy, the expression is probably healthy. If it is unhealthy, or if the response is *inappropriate*, we will usually feel unhappiness.

Even the criteria "happy/unhappy" has drawbacks when we attempt discovery of love/hate relationships on our own. While it *can* be done through deep introspection and understanding of our emotional responses, recognition of inappropriate expressions may be illusive. On such a deep survival-oriented subject, those love/hate responses that have been distorted may not feel either happy *or unhappy* when we investigate them. Their distortion has caused them to *appear different* than they actually are. Once again, our subjective vision is hampered by *closeness to the source*.

Perhaps the most efficient means of achieving recognition of destructive love/hate is through collective investigation. Our emotional responses to love/hate are of such intensity that we can rarely hide them from the presence *of others*. Love/hate creates a certain distinct expression on our faces, an aura about us that everyone can see. Destructive love/hate creates an impression that just doesn't seem *appropriate* in context with the subject. Inappropriate, destructive love/hate *looks* obviously different. Objective interpretation of the difference often leads to the discovery of inappropriate love/hate.

Once we discover which love/hate responses are uncalled for, we need to recognize the stereotype that gave rise to it. When we have done those two things, we can once again return to *spontaneous* response in *appropriate* reaction. When we have destroyed the distortion, we will feel *relieved* of our stereotypical burden and be able to *feel good* about expressing healthy hate against someone we are conditioned *to believe we should love*. Without the stereotypes and other distortion, our love/hate becomes *unaffected and spontaneous*.

Collective investigation and introspection each contribute to eliminating destructive love/hate. When we have gotten rid of this cause of emotional distress, we can replace it with *appropriate, healthy* reactions.

After discovering the affected relationships and bringing them into conscious awareness, we can then replace them with pro-survival responses that *enhance* our well being instead of *destroying* it. In this way, constructive love/hate creates contentment.

<u>PRODUCTIVE FANTASY LIFE</u>

In the section on the causes of misery, much was made of the importance of creative imagination and mental relaxation. The cure to the distress caused by lack of relaxation is one of the most simple and, at the same time, enjoyable discoveries we can make.

When we daydream, we are in the act of fantasying, allowing the mind to wander at will. It is generally the case that this mental relaxation comes at a time of mental stress. We fantasize more during an important lesson in school than when our attention is required less, our thoughts less forced and our enjoyment more. Daydreaming, in this way, acts as a release valve when stress comes along.

A block to productive fantasies is fear, often times a severe phobic reaction. Many people, either consciously or *below their awareness*, are afraid that fantasies lead inevitably to loss of control, the inability to differentiate between the real and unreal worlds. Others might believe that fantasy is an "escape" from reality, an escape from the here-and-now, and like *all escapes*, they think are bad. There are many other fears, stereotypes and misinformation that sometimes block the ability to fantasize.

Healthy fantasies present no obstacle to healthy, well-organized rational thinking. In the sense that it is a trip toward relaxation, toward nothing but non-structured thought processing, escape can be as healthy as it is pro-survival. There is no possibility of "going crazy" through a healthy fantasy life. Only if the fantasies are used because phobias, stereotypes or other unhealthy reactions distort their influence and turn fantasy into inappropriate reality, could there be a problem. On their own, for their own purpose, fantasies offer the release we all need for optimum functioning.

The process of building productive fantasies, or maintaining their effectiveness if we've already improved our *natural inclination*, is fun. "Getting away from it all," "Going somewhere else," are typical phrases we use when planning a vacation. Fantasies are another non-physical vacation, a trip we can take without moving our physical body. It is a fulfilling release of tension.

Creative imagination is the ability to design our thoughts for some specific purpose, perhaps to come up with a solution to a problem in some novel way, uniquely our own. In fantasy building, this ability comes in handy. By using creative imagination, we can organize thoughts, translate them, change mental imagery, or develop a specific fulfilling fantasy. Creative imagination, properly employed, can help us greatly in the pursuit of productive fantasy.

While creative imagination can be of tremendous assistance in building our non-material, non-rational world, it is only a stepping stone to the end goal. It can certainly be a separate form of fantasy life, a *directed* activity with *specific* rules and methods, but creative imagination requires energy. Even though the process is very rewarding *on its own*, one of the most important uses of, and reason for, fantasy is realization. Using any kind of energy lessens the relaxing effect.

Once we develop the ability to "get away from it all," we can then break all the rules and allow the mind free reign to trip where and how it wants. While it spins its web of irrational, illogical thought patterns, visual and auditory images, colors, designs, and sounds, we can just sit back and *let it be* and allow it freedom. We can just watch our fantasies, observe them objectively, without feeling *obligated* to control them or influence where they are headed.

Besides allowing the mind a much-needed rest from dealing with demanding here-and-now, fantasies also allow a glimpse into the inner workings of the subconscious. While we watch the fantastical world go by on parade, we can often recognize important images or thoughts and allow those memories to come together and interact *without our direction*. By seeing how situations develop and work themselves out, either beneficially or negatively, we can observe those factors that influence our emotional responses. It may be necessary to remove some of the more destructive ideas. After allowing memory to *just be*, we can often times develop a much keener awareness of thought patterns and their relative importance in our emotional functioning.

Fantasies come in many types and sizes. Through sexual fantasies, we can increase physical, emotional and spiritual release in a constructive manner. Alone or with others, fantasy can *enhance our enjoyment*. Further fantasy offers the ultimate freedom for the mind; liberation from the bondage of reason and logic.

Creative imagination has a secure niche in the world of non-rational, non-logical, non-material mental functioning. It is a separate *directed* form of fantasy. On the other side of the coin is *total detachment*. Just allow our fantasies to journey wherever they might and to *direct themselves* from beginning to end.

Forms of release, creative imagination and detached fantasy are healthy and life enhancing. However, when combined for the improper reasons, as a *habitual* escape, for example, or when reality becomes excessively distressful, fantasy can act in concert with unhealthy emotional reactions, actually resulting in severe mental illness. It has nothing to do with *fantasy itself*. Only the *unhealthy interactions* are at fault. In all other respects, unless fantasies are used in these or similar *unhealthy ways*, they are natural and life enhancing.

Fantasies can safely involve the unspeakable. Through building our interior, private world and allowing it freedom of direction or using creative imagination, we can do the impossible. Using fantasy as a relaxation technique, a way of "letting go," we can do what we always wanted to do but wouldn't (read couldn't). We can safely do that which would be against physical or emotional survival if we acted it out in our material existence.

Because those things which we are normally inhibited from doing are very powerful, fantasy can relieve intense built-up pressure and make our dealings with the world much easier and more beneficial.

Hallucinations are another, more intense and commanding, form of fantasy. Even though this type of fantasy combines the real and imaginative worlds, superimposing them upon each other until fantasy and reality *are one*, they are nevertheless sometimes healthy. However, *acting them out* could be *counter-productive*. Behaving as per our fantasized role is often *unhealthy* since that action many times deals with doing the *unspeakable*. In fantasy, we run no risk of encountering a real threat to our survival, while in the real world, that threat could possibly lead to our self-destruction. Hallucinations most times are relaxing and interesting. Hallucinations sometimes become intense beyond coping and we may act out the self-destructive fantasy. Other than acting out, fantasy is healthy.

Hand in hand with mental relaxation goes concommitant relaxation in the other two spheres. Allowing the body to *do nothing but just be* relieves all sorts of built-up pressures and enhances optimum functioning on all levels. Fantasies offer a form of relaxation that is more all-inclusive than relaxation designed to benefit any one of the other spheres alone.

Through creative imagination and directed growth, we can overcome blocks to fantasy building. A productive fantasy life, originating in the emotional sphere of being, brings with it spiritual and physical contentment.

For life is the mirror of king and slave,
'Tis just what we are and do.
—Madeline Bridges

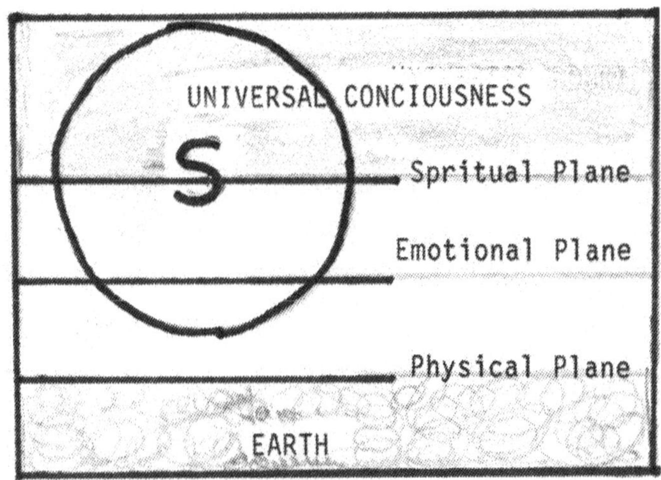

ILLUSTRATION 10

SPIRITUAL CURES

MEDITATION/REALIZATION

Concentration, comprehension, understanding the inner workings of our consciousness, are by-products and consequences of stilling the mind. Calming mental functioning, simply allowing subconscious images to surface where we can analyze and define them aids in understanding the nature of phobias, stereotypes, and even creative imagination. This stilling of the mind, combined with focusing awareness, intensifies what is already beneath awareness and makes it more accessible.

Stilling the mind, as mentioned earlier, can be accomplished through yoga training. Rhythmic breathing (using what is called "prana"—the key to our *essence*) helps relaxation of body, mind and spirit. Controlled breathing, while directing thought, increases concentration, resulting in a deeper awareness of the subconscious. Concentration requires psychic energy, so the mind cannot be *entirely stilled* this way. Mental functioning becomes slower, more efficient and is more acute. Yet *completely stilling the mind* is impossible when thoughts are being consciously analyzed. So, while concentration and reverie aid in investigation, they require *too much work*. Another method needs to be found for spiritual discovery.

Meditation, another regimen, is usually begun in the same way as concentration, through consciously controlled breathing, directing thought patterns, and then the complete stilling of mental and emotional functioning. There are many ways of achieving contact with the super-conscious realm— chanting uses physical sound to aid in relaxation, to stop images, thoughts and reverie form influencing the mind. Body posture from the "full lotus" position where feet are crossed upon the thighs while seated, to sitting straight-backed in a chair, to lying prone, has an effect on the depth of meditation.

Body posture increases awareness primarily because it keeps aches and pains caused by muscle tension from entering consciousness. If there is no tension and if the body is completely relaxed, relieving *physical awareness* becomes easier. Rhythmic breathing increases the flow of oxygen to the brain, which has a pronounced effect on slowing conscious functioning. Chanting, incense and a myriad of other accouterments enhance relaxation, making it easier to achieve.

Once the body and mind are stilled as much as possible, the primary point of meditation becomes attainable. Without effort, allowing the spiritual sphere to reach out of the material world, into its own Universal Consciousness, we contact the highest realm of *being*. The spiritual sphere siphons some of the highly charged positivity of the super-conscious information. When we once again restore full mental activity by stopping meditation, that energy will have been channeled into *conscious awareness*. After contact, we are filled with new energy and *feel great*!

The reason stilling the mind is imperative to spiritual travel is that any distraction from the other spheres hampers *total* spiritual freedom. Since it functions in another dimension, the spirit has different needs from consciousness. Its workings are much more complex and delicate. With no distractions to affect it, the spiritual sphere can attain oneness with Universal Consciousness.

In a union with *pure essence*, the spiritual sphere is in contact with all that has ever been, will be or *is*. It is one with *being*, the essence of *all*. In this highest dimension, where *all* coexists, the spirit is not a *part of all*, it *is* all. It therefore has the ability to channel information about its being, about the higher dimension, back down into the lower spheres.

In esoteric literature which tries to deal through words with another dimension that is *beyond language*, symbols are always necessary to convey perceptions. The super-conscious is beyond words, so words try vainly to bring that dimension into experiential terms. In every major religion, philosophy, or concept, a thread of identity interconnects them. In everything that *is*, the identical concepts of Universal Consciousness are symbolized by words in different ways to make ordinary beings understand.

Symbols of highest Beings range from *God* to *Allah* to *Jehovah* in Western religions to Super-consciousness in the East. But, the same concepts exist in all the symbols. They are only different ways of expressing the idea of Universal Consciousness. Likewise, deification of a concept, the ideas of *Heaven,* or the *Netherworld,* are symbolic expressions of the highest dimension, when spirit separates from the body and rejoins its essence in Universal Consciousness. Christians, for example, talk of "going to heaven" when they die. In concept, it is identical to returning to Universal Consciousness when spirit and body separate. Universal Consciousness is no more than another *symbol* to express the concept, but it has less religious stigma and negative associations related to "belief," which is a matter of *opinion* rather than *reason.* At any rate, it is not the word, but *the concept,* which matters.

All beings coexist with, inside, and of itself and *everything* simultaneously. Spirit is Universal Consciousness, though it is unusually constrained of its traveling freedom as the cup separates the water from the pool. While in the physical body, spirit receives energy from the material plane to establish spiritual growth.

Meditation releases the spiritual being from the body for a brief temporal moment. The constraint of material existence is temporarily removed and the spiritual sphere is able, temporarily, to rejoin Universal Consciousness. It is as if the water in the cup was symbolically joined through a hollow straw to the pool. While still separated by the cup, the water is able to contact its essence in the pool.

As mentioned earlier, sexual expression is one of the most important instincts we have. It can create a major spiritual cure as well. During orgasm, we achieve temporary union with Universal Consciousness. Although orgasm lasts only a brief moment, the peak of ecstasy when all body tension is explosively released, we nevertheless, for that instant, contact the highest dimension. Sexual expression carries with it a concomitant *spiritual experience.*

Tantric Yoga and *Tantric Buddhism* are branches of the larger movements that detail methods for achieving orgasmic ecstatic spiritual experience. These schools of philosophical thought recognize that sexual expression can be a method of achieving contact with Universal Consciousness. Through differing forms of sexual body postures combined with deep meditation and intense sensory input, a deep spiritual experience and accompanying contact with the highest dimension fulfills spiritual, emotional and physical needs.

In both meditation by itself and through sexual expression, Realization is the process of becoming one with Universal Consciousness. When our consciousness is permeated with *pure being,* when we have come to a *total awareness* of spiritual matters *beyond* mere understanding or comprehension, or when we are super-conscious, awareness of the highest dimension allows us to speed up spiritual growth, cast off physical existence for the last time and end the necessity of multiple manifestations on the material plane. When we are *one with Universal Consciousness*, we are *Realized*.

Realization comes ultimately when we terminate physical existence for the final time, when we have achieved ultimate spiritual growth, when we reach spiritual perfection. Through meditation and accelerating spiritual growth, our need for multiple existence vanishes. Through contact with the highest dimension, we can more quickly attain Realization.

When using words, all we can hope to do is come to a *general understanding* of the concepts. Through meditation and merging with Universal Consciousness, even temporarily, words are no longer needed. Expression of words is unnecessary. Through contact with Universal Consciousness, we achieve *spontaneous knowledge*.

Through even partial stilling of the mind, improved concentration/comprehension and many other abilities that enhance our survival are possible. But, *partial* stilling is not *complete spiritual freedom*. Meditation allows conscious awareness of either the physical or emotional spheres. Spiritual being naturally tends to merge with Universal Consciousness during meditation.

Through super-conscious contact, the spiritual is all problems, *all* answers, *ALL*. Meditation, by allowing the freedom to contact, channels the essence of what was, is and will be into our awareness. We solve problems through *spontaneous knowledge*. They simply *solve themselves*. After full contact, after merging with Universal Consciousness even briefly, we see our place in the scheme of things in a different, more serious, yet less disturbing light. Realization is, in effect, a realization of who, what, when, how, and why of existence.

Meditation leads not only to Realization, but less than the ultimate, to increased self-image, emotional stability, even physical well being. We achieve "calm in the face of the storm." By merging spiritual essence with the essence of being, *all things are possible*. Perfection is approached. In this way, while enhancing spiritual development, the benefit is felt throughout. Meditation alleviates distress in all three spheres of being.

<u>INCREASED PSYCHIC PERCEPTION</u>

Since so much subliminal information comes into our subconscious store, when we do not recognize it as such, its usefulness is lost. Without knowing which memories are actually psychic perceptions, there are subtle influences on our thinking/responses. Full conscious awareness of them not only makes analysis easier, but also allows enhanced ability to receive/transmit psychic information.

The first step toward increased psychic perception is becoming aware of which perceptions come through the physical senses (smells, tastes, sights, sounds, and feelings) and which come through higher extrasensory awareness. The difference is not always as obvious as it might seem.

If we meet someone who we feel is "nice," his/her features may be soft, friendly, or "nice." Our physical perceptions, what we *see,* may be the basis of our judgment. On the other hand, at times we meet people whose features are hard, unfriendly, even hostile, yet we feel they are nice *in spite of* their appearance. At these times, it may be the *aura* of the person, the psychic energy field surrounding their physical being, which is positive and is conveyed to the subconscious as useful information in character judgment. In either case, we perceive the person similarly, as "nice," although one judgment came through what we physically observed while the other arrived through a higher sense of which we may usually remain unaware.

Being aware of psychic perception in the above example may not be imperative. It may make no difference if we *know* that the judgment was based upon extrasensory information since the response that we had to the person *enhanced our well being.* However, should we instead come across someone to whom we might react negatively although outward appearances would suggest a positive reaction is in order, the psychic perception of ill-feeling will cause distress. By recognizing that the judgment, in fact, has a psychic origin, that it is a perception and not of the physical person, but of his/her spiritual radiation, we could avoid that unnecessary distress.

Awareness of the aura and the ability to perceive it is necessary to deciphering subconscious information. Besides the psychic radiation surrounding the being, psychic perceptions also include some other so-called "psychic phenomena."

The most common psychic phenomena with which we come into daily contact are of telepathic origin. One can pick up energy transmitted consciously or unconsciously from one being to another. At times we get a "feeling" that someone is unhappy, worried or is thinking of some vague idea although we have no other way to know such things. We rarely recognize that these perceptions are reflections of psychic energy that we have picked up from another person's psychic force field. Yet they seriously affect our conscious analysis.

Thoughts are little more than electrochemical reactions in the brain. Chemistry causes electric conduction from one cell to another and the connection causes thought. Likewise, electrochemical reactions are responsible for associations. But, besides electricity and chemistry, the emotions deal partially in the spiritual sphere of being and thus contain some energy that is non-material. It is similar to electricity with a definable field of current, wavelength, pattern, a specific strength. But this energy is immeasurable by scientific quantative analysis. It defies compartmentalization in mainstream science. Yet psychic energy is responsible for transmitting thought patterns *outside* the mind.

Television is a complicated, though understandable, physical phenomenon. Using it as a symbolic comparison, psychic energy is easier to visualize. Like television transmission, psychic information is also a form of energy. The mind is the transmitter while *spiritual/psychic essence* is the medium (like television waves). At the other end of the transmission is the television set which translates the microwaves back into electrical signals that are shown on the television screen. Similarly, psychic information is received by another being and translated into subliminal data on which to base a judgment about them.

Of course, television works through physical laws while psychic perceptions deal in another dimension. But, they are similar in their mechanics. The cause-and-effect relationship is the same. They are both in the electromagnetic spectrum. An investigation of the coincidences of the two types of energy results in even keener understanding of psychic transmission and reception.

Television is received by many sets from one transmission point. Psychic information is likewise received by many other beings from one projection of psychic energy. Before the television's microwave transmission is translated into a visible image and while it is still in the set's circuitry, the picture is invisible. It has not yet been recreated. In the mind, the same is true. Psychic information remains invisible in the subconscious until it is retrieved to awareness for some practical judgmental use. After the signals are assembled into recognizable form, the true origin of both forms is unrecognizable. Microwaves become visible images with no sign of being an electronic conversion. Psychic information simply becomes conscious memory with no attached psychic origin.

The need for an awareness of psychic perceptions is clear, but the method is happily less complex. The process of increasing psychic perceptibility has several beneficial by-products. For one thing, we can increase our natural ability for transmitting psychic energy to another being, establishing at least a one-way telepathic link. Our reception ability likewise increases so we are better able to develop a *double link* if the other person can develop a similar ability. Reception also means that we are better able to translate other psychic data into conscious awareness. Precognition might make us aware of coming events that are important to our survival. Clairvoyance may make us better able to "breach the beyond" and contact the essences of people who have been liberated from the material plane. Many and various psychic perceptions become capable of being formed, transmitted, received, and understood through increased ability.

Experimenting with the increased development of psychic perception is enjoyable. Since experimentation can bring with it an enhanced ability to *get closer to people*, to really understand *where they're coming from* and why they appear to us as they do, developing psychic perception adds immeasurably to interpersonal relations. For example, during a party we may be able to meet someone we are attracted to without having to introduce ourselves. Or, during sexual expressions, words become unnecessary to convey our desires. In every day functions, increasing psychic perceptibility is great fun!

For many reasons, becoming more aware of which of our perceptions are actually psychic in origin, greatly increases our enjoyment of the extrasensory world surrounding us. There is an abundance of information that may truly aid our continued success in life. Or, it might be merely entertaining and fun. Psychic energy, in short, is as varied as the essences of many other people manifesting through our reception.

Because of the ability to contact, translate, and comprehend necessary information, spiritually bringing it into awareness and using subliminal data for improving our well being, increased psychic perception enhances life and directly creates contentment in all three spheres of being.

EFFECTIVE COMMUNICATION

Communication is by far the most important part of our interactions. In it lies the major interaction we have with our environment and with ourselves.

The several complex, omnipresent problems that result from ineffective communication were briefly discussed under "Causes." Suffice that they are of utmost concern and cause severe unnecessary distress. That the effects can be devastating is fact. Now it is time to see the *benefits* of *effective* communication.

When we are able to express ourselves fully, to make our wants, desires, concerns, and emotions understood by those to whom we express them, we open a "channel of communication." When someone fully appreciates what we are saying, how and why we feel as we do, it becomes much easier, more satisfying, to be a *part of our world*. They find expressing themselves *to us* easier. We allow them to *communicate* with us. We communicate *with them*. Together we effectively bridge the "communication gap."

There are many forms of communication as mentioned earlier. The most recognizable, perhaps, is *speech*. *Saying what we mean* and *meaning what we say* (sincerity) communicate some of our important verbal thoughts, ideas and emotions. Speech is a method of communication.

Then there are *non*-verbal communications. We express tenderness by touching. Desire is sometimes expressed by caring, fondling, or holding another person. Gentleness, caring, love, and happiness we communicate most effectively in non-verbal ways, not using words. Similarly, we express anger, irritation, surprise, and a host of other emotions (both positive and negative and those in between) through non-verbal communication.

In collective investigation of our inner processes, communication plays an important role. If we express ourselves fully, if we communicate, the other people involved in the process will more fully understand us. In addition, a little basic knowledge of the general concepts involved in *body language becomes* obvious. For instance, if our facial expressions, when describing a love affair, communicate disgust instead of delight, it may appear inappropriate to others. If it isn't appropriate, our non-verbal communication will have defined a subconscious memory that has influenced our lives fallaciously.

The way we hold our head, hands and legs when talking to others are other non-verbal postures which sometimes communicate how we feel about what we are saying. Some of our postures have little to do with inappropriate responses.

In implementing the cure to serious spiritual distress, there are several prime spots of focus. The first of these is *verbal* communication. Through collective investigation, others can watch us objectively and, at the proper time, call our attention to the ways we communicate verbally. Thus, we begin to learn to express ourselves more fully, to the benefit of all concerned.

When increasing effective verbal communication, we need to be especially concerned with those we care about. By *expressing ourselves, sharing* our concerns and emotions, and our love, we not only open a "channel of communication," but also strengthen viable relationships.

Finally, many people have a major block to free and open communication when it comes to *touching*. Stereotypes are most often responsible for this communications breakdown. "Men *shouldn't* hug each other." "You *shouldn't* (read: *under no circumstances can*) touch someone *there*!" There are many built-up associations and stigmas connected to this most important part of human communication.

We all need to be touched, held, and stroked to be healthy. Scientific studies have shown an undeniable connection between the amount of "stroking behavior" in humans and other animals and *emotional well being*. Those animals who openly express themselves most often through touching are consistently more emotionally stable, secure, happy and more physically healthy than those who maintained physical "distance."

Hugging is a warm, healthy expression of our regard for someone. A hand on the shoulder, or ours on another, expresses warmth, sincerity, and honesty. Intense emotions we could not communicate with words alone. Caressing signifies strong caring love. All "stroking behavior" shows we *care* about each other. Without it, we don't know to what *extent* we feel. But, through non-verbal stroking, we effectively communicate the *intensity* of our emotions.

Of course, stereotypes, phobias and other unhealthy emotional associations must be gotten rid of before optimum communication can take place. But, such simple human warmth as is communicated by a hug, caress, or a stroke is a big help to that end. Sincerity and honesty enhance the freedom of expression.

When we learn to communicate effectively, we will have successfully bridged the "communication gap." We are then able to make ourselves understood, understand others, and empathize with them and *share ourselves* unselfishly. Through verbal and non-verbal means we can implement the cures.

Since it is most necessary to the success of the other cures, effective communication is, by rights, of primary importance. By increasing effective communication we create simultaneous well being in all three spheres.

<u>ON THE CURES; A CONCLUSION</u>

Just as the "Causes" in Part 1 barely breached the surface of a deeper morass of distressful situations, so also are the ten cures here presented not the *entire gamut*.

Effective communication aids in the implementation of gymnosophy, increased vitality, healthy sexual expression in the physical sphere of being, elimination of phobic reactions, reduction of stereotypes, constructive love/hate and productive fantasy life in the emotional, along with Meditation/Realization and increased psychic perceptions in the spiritual sphere. Overall, communication aids in discovery and investigation of distress throughout.

While these are *the ten most important* of the myriad cures, there are many others which are unique to the individual. Some people will have causes that apply *only to them*.

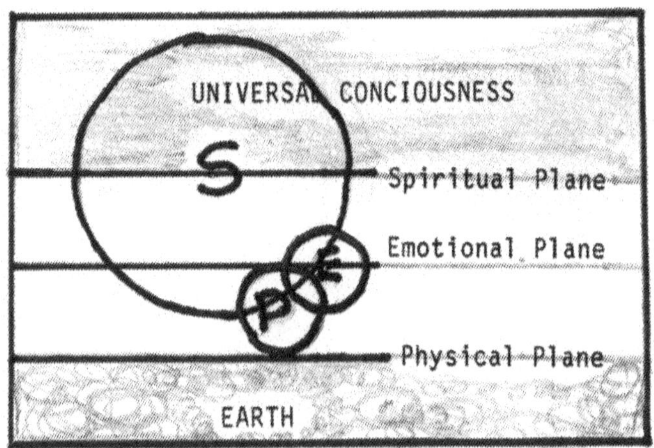

<u>ILLUSTRATION 11</u>

Obviously, there are as many possible causes for individual misery as there are individuals. So are unique cures. There will be some people who read this book that will find very little which applies specifically to them. Others will identify more of the ten as causes of their personal misery, and will then have more use for the consequent cures. But, even if there is *only one* cause presented here and *only one cure*, the book will have achieved its goal.

Everything in this book, all thought, all opinions and all discussion has been presented for a single overwhelming purpose. Through reading, understanding, using the methods and analysis of cause-and-cure found here, many will finally achieve

72

<u>THE CONQUEST OF MISERY.</u>

PART 3:
THE CHURCH

Philosophy should be an energy; it
Should find its aim and its effect in the
Amelioration of mankind.
—Victor Hugo

Since the purpose of this book, and the presentation of ten major causes and cures, is the elimination of misery from this planet, simply *discussing* the subject without an adequate means for assisting in individual discovery would be pointless. A means for implementing the cures and disseminating information on the causes is a necessity. Without such a system, finding cures and uncovering causes would be merely a stimulating, intellectual exercise. Direction of concerted effort greatly enhances the probability of success.

The Church of Psychic Sanctuary is the organization to that end.

The Church is a "religion" as that word is literally defined. It is an "organized system of belief." But there, with the basic definition, the similarity to other religions ends.

Unlike most others, The Church of Psychic Sanctuary has no religious dogma. There is no concept that members are *obliged* to accept. Rather, The Church encourages individual discovery and analysis of ideas. If, after using reason and logic, the concepts seem valid to the member, he/she can accept them. If, on the other hand, they are personally not useful, he/she can simply dismiss them. The individual freedom of choice is stressed above all other communication.

Another lack of similarity to other organized religions is in The Church's concept of morality. By replacing "should/shouldn't" and "shall/shall not" with the more practical "healthy/unhealthy," members can make a unique choice, an individual, highly personalized morality.

The determination of morality encouraged by The Church is basically this: *If, after weighing the facts, you decide that your proposed action is healthy for you and does not violate the freedoms of another, the action can be safely considered "moral.'* However, the whole point of an individual determination is to get away from stereotypes. Therefore, because of the unhealthy stigma attached to them, the words "moral" and "immoral" are discouraged. They are to be replaced by an emphasis on "healthy" or "unhealthy" *consequences.*

There are seven members on the Board of Directors who ensure the smooth operation of The Church, its effectiveness as a method of implementation of various cures and its overall success.

The men and women who form the Directorship are mutually responsible for ensuring that The Church will always be responsive to the needs of its members, and that it will always be able to easily change whenever necessary. Its continued success in eliminating misery is thus assured. Members can change *Church Policy* without the Directors' permission. The Directorship initiates more subtle, practical alterations of direction, but the members have equal power.

There are Ministers, Teachers and many other dedicated Church workers whose primary interest is in the ultimate success of The Church. The elimination of misery from this planet is their main incentive, their driving motivation.

The Church is more a reflection of its members than a static entity. It is a living being, collective consciousness in organized form. As the needs of the members change, so does the Church. It is vital and dynamic. It serves the members instead of the members serving The Church, another difference between The Church of Psychic Sanctuary and many other organizations.

Even the name says a lot about what it represents. "Psychic" is that part of the being that is concerned with the higher functions of mind and super-physical impressions. "Sanctuary" is a safe place to be, a retreat where you feel secure against harm. The Church of Psychic Sanctuary represents a place where you can be safe to use your higher functions as you see fit. It is somewhere to feel secure with doing what you know is healthy instead of what others say you *should* do.

The elimination of misery from this planet is its ultimate goal. When The Church of Psychic Sanctuary achieves perfection, when misery in the world is no more, its purpose will have vanished. Like the perfected spirit, the collective organization of The Church will merge its essence into Universal Consciousness. With no misery left to be cured, it will naturally cease to exist.

The Church of Psychic Sanctuary is a growing, vibrant being and is available to all who are sincerely interested in improving their lives and increasing their potential for happiness.

Whether you wish to become involved in The Church, whether you decide to investigate your personal misery on your own, or whether you have disagreed with the entire premise of this book, by reading it and accepting its contents even as "possibly true", you are well on your way to helping achieve a noble purpose. You will have begun your journey to perfection. And you will have begun your personal

<u>CONQUEST OF MISERY.</u>

1962
1974 Revised
1998 Revised
2001 Revised

<u>GLOSSARY</u>

Apropos-Fitting; suitable; to the point

Asana-Hindu word denoting a particular body posture used in yogic exercise (see also *Yoga*)

Association-A mental connection established by a process of learning; a connection by virtue of social conditioning

Au Naturel-French adverb denoting a natural condition; particularly in the nude

Brain-The physical organ which uses electrochemical action to make connections for activating the various body functions (for corollary, see *Mind)*

Church-A group of people involved in a common spiritual pursuit; a collective religious organization

Codified-Systematized; made into an established code; *as laws are codified morals*; morals systematized into an established code of conduct

Collective Awareness Development-A group of people involved in the common effort of investigating their attitudes toward life, their problems, and developing their individual awareness through interaction with others

Communication-From the Latin prefix "com", meaning with, together in conjunction with; it is a word that denotes the interchange of thoughts or opinions; *effective communication* implies that the interchange is successful on both sides; that understanding is complete

Concomitant-Also from the Latin prefix "con" (the same origin as "com"), signifying that two things go together; accompanying; conjoined

Creative Imagination-The ability to formulate mental images which are not from outside; the act of using fantasy for creative solution to problems; the ability to let the mind run free while attaining measurable results of mental functioning

Daydream-A non-controlled fantasy in which mental images come of their own accord; a non-directed fantasy

Empathy-Feeling as if the problems of another are one's own; intense identification of self with another

Escape-By definition, the avoidance of a threatened ill; evasion of injury by removing oneself from the potential problem; *in practice*, taking a "vacation" from worry

Extra-A Latin prefix that denotes beyond, outside of, outside the scope of; as in *extraordinary*, meaning beyond the parameters of physical senses; from another sensibility

Fallacy-A false idea; reason which fails to satisfy the requirements of logical proof; violating validity; an untrue supposition

Fantasy-A product of imagination; an illusory image; a phantasm; a mental image or series of images generated completely from within the mind by its own internal power

Group-The same as "collective", the word denotes more than two people pursuing the same goal; an assemblage of more than two people

Gymnosophy-From the words "gymnos" (Greek, meaning uncovered, nude) and "sophos" (Greek, meaning wisdom), it is an ancient philosophy concerning the benefits of social nudism

Hallucination-A form of fantasy in which imagination and reality become mixed and the differences between the two vanish; a fantasy which is often indistinguishable by the halluucinator from that which he perceives outside himself

Healthy-Conducive to soundness of mind or body; freedom from illness or distress (for opposite, see *unhealthy*)

-ism-A Latin suffix that changes the intention of the word it modifies to mean a manner of action, conduct characteristic of the group or person named; attachment or adherence to some idea or concept; as adherence to belief of The Church of England, Anglician*ism*; often denotes fanatical attachment to a fallacious stereotype, as in rac*ism*, sex*ism*

Love/Hate-An emotional expression somewhere between the extremes of *complete toward* (love) and *completely against* (hate) a person or object; a combining emotion which is more realistic and common than either love or hate alone

Manifestation-Being obvious to the senses; appearing on the material plane; becoming concrete, as in birth

Mind-The non-physical functions of the brain that control reason, logic, interpretation of incoming data; controller of the higher mental functions; next to emotions in strength and complexity of work (for corollary, see *Brain*)

Morality-A systemized collection of principles dealing with the *rightness* or *wrongness* of actions; a conception of good or bad action based on non-individual social value judgments

Natural-Innate; inborn; the ways we react without social conditioning or any other influence; expression without regard to stereotype or other inhibitors of spontaneity, (for opposite, see *Unnatural)*

Omnivorous-Denotes the human capacity to eat all kinds of foods as opposed to *carni*vorous (meat-eating) or *herbi*vorous (vegetation-eating)

Phobia-A negative over-reaction of terror to an occurrence to which are attached unnecessary fears; fallacious responses to circumstances based upon associations between once-healthy fear and incidental occurrences

Planes of Existence-In esoteric philosophy, the varying levels or degrees of complexity of the human being; usually three planes of existence are accepted—Physical, Mental, and Spiritual (variously called Super-conscious, Soul, etc.); Identical in content to Physical, Emotional and Spiritual *spheres of being*

Private-Denotes that those present share the same attitudes, ideas and opinions about the action they are involved in as a group (for opposite, see *Public)*

Provocateur-One who excites; arouses to action; incites. Also a thing which stimulates reaction

Psychic-Having to do with the higher, non-material level of functioning; those abilities of a non-physical nature that deal directly through the third sphere of being

Public-Denotes that those present do not share the same ideas, attitudes or opinions; that they are dissimilar in many ways, and do not accept behavior that, by the larger society, is considered anti-social or in any way detrimental to the large group (for opposite, see *Private)*

Realization-Instantaneous knowledge of all wisdom; the total understanding, comprehension of all the Mysteries of Life; oneness with Universal Consciousness

Religion-An organized system of belief; the practice of deep commitment to and comprehension of a higher level of existence than of this planet

Sanctuary-Asylum; a place of safety from attack; a secure place to just *be*

Social Convention-An accepted form of behavior that has been acknowledged by the society to be correct when in public; in the presence of the general population; an agreed behavior; a way of conducting oneself in social situations

Spheres of Being-Differing levels of complexity of function of the human being, from the most basic, the Physical to the higher Emotional to the highest level, the Spiritual. Identical in content to Physical, Mental and Spiritual *planes of existence*

Spontaneity-Action without deliberation; response without influence of unhealthy emotional associations; proceeding from natural, innate feeling without constraint; action based solely upon internal impulse; natural free expression

Stereotype-An expected result based upon fallacious information; an expectation resulting from identification of groups of individuals as non-individuals; an unrealistic judgment based on ignorance of individual traits

Sub-A prefix denoting below, as in *sub*marines travel *below* the water

Super-A prefix denoting above, over, as *super*human describes powers which are above, over those normally associated with humans

Sympathy-An affinity with another which makes one feel similarly to the other; strong identification between individuals; reciprocal affection due to similarities

Trans-A prefix denoting across, as transcontinental describes *across* the continent

Transactional Analysis-A process of group therapy, collective investigation in which the human personality is seen as consisting of three integrated parts, the Child (natural instincts), Adult (reasoning and mental functioning) and Parent (the association of the content of learned behavior) which interact and affect each other's functioning

Unhealthy-Destructive to mind or body; susceptible to illness; in a state of being non-conducive to health (for opposite, see *Healthy*)

Universal Consciousness-The ultimate level of existence in another dimension; without physical presence; the essence of all that is, has been, or will be

Unnatural-Affected actions based upon unhealthy social conditioning; expression which is influenced by negative emotional associations; inhibited from being spontaneous (for opposite, *Natural*)

Yin/Yang-The Eastern philosophy of the similarity/dissimilarity of things where *yin* denotes the white, pure, clean, day side of life while *yang* denotes evil, black, unclean, the night side. Most experiences lie somewhere between the extremes of *yin* and *yang* in *yin/yang*

Yoga-A discipline directed primarily toward spiritual attainment with regimens for developing good health, sound emotional equilibrium and spiritual perfection through interactions of all three parts of being

BIBLIOGRAPHY

BOOKS FUNDAMENTAL TO THE CHURCH OF PSYCHIC SANCTUARY

1. Heinlein, Robert A STRANGER IN A STRANGE LAND, New York, Putnam (1961) 408 p.

2. Harris, Thomas Anthony I'M OK—YOU'RE OK A Practical Guide to Transactional Analysis, Boston, G. K. HALL (1974) 554 p.

3. Huxley, Aldous BRAVE NEW WORLD, New York, Perennial Classics (1998) 270 p.

4. Masters, William H. and Johnson, Virginia E. HUMAN SEXUAL RESPONSE, Boston, Little, Brown (1966) 366 p.

5. Morris, Desmond THE NAKED APE: A Zoologist's Study of the Human Animal New York, McGraw-Hill (1967) 252 p.

6. Gibran, Khalil THE PROPHET New York, Knopf (1968) 98 p.

7. THE BIBLE Chicago, University of Chicago Press (1931) 1,619 p.

8. Rendered Into English by Syed Abdul Latif al QURAN Hyderadan, India Academy of Islamic Studies (1969) 579 p.

9. Watts, Alan BECOME WHAT YOUR ARE Boston, Shambhala (1995) 127 p.

10. Durant, Will THE STORY OF PHILOSOPHY: The Lives and Opinions of the Great Philosophers of the Western World New York (1983) 412 p.

BOOKS RELATIVE TO CAUSES AND CURES OF MISERY

BODY FREEDOM

11. Hartman, William E. NUDIST SOCIETY: The Controversial Study of the Clothes-Free Naturist Movement in America Revised and Updated by Iris Bancroft, Los Angeles, Elysium Growth Press (1991) 478 p.

12. Parmelee, Maurice Farr <u>NATURISM IN MODERN LIFE: The New Gymnosophy</u> Mays Landing, NJ, Sunshine Book Company (1941) 303 p.

<u>DIET/NUTRITION/HEALTH</u>

13. Peterkin, Betty B. <u>FOOD SELECTION FOR GOOD NUTRITION FOR GROUP FEEDING</u> Washington, Agricultural Research Service, U. S. Department of Agriculture (1968) 32 p.

14. Ward, Bryan R. <u>DIET AND NUTRITION</u> London and New York, F. Watts (1987) 48 p.

<u>SEXUALITY</u>

15. Wikoff, Johanina <u>THE COMPLETE IDIOT'S GUIDE TO THE KAMA SUTRA</u> Indianapolis, Alpha Books (2000) 362 p.

16. Shah, Pragna R. <u>TANTRA, ITS THERAPEUTIC ASPECT</u> Calcutta, Punthi Purtak (1987) 161 p.

17. Elisofom, Eliot <u>EROTIC SPIRITUALITY: The Vision of Konarak</u>, With Commentary by Alan Watts, New York, Collins Books (1974) 174 p.

18. Williams, Mark J. K. <u>SEXUAL PATHWAYS: Adapting to Dual Sexual Attraction</u> Westport, Ct, Praeger (1999) 179 p.

19. Frost, Gavin <u>TANTRIC YOGA, THE ROYAL PATH TO RAISING KUNDALINI POWER</u> York Beach, ME (1989) 306 p.

20. Masters, R. E. L. <u>SEXUAL SELF-STIMULATION</u> Los Angeles, Sherbourne Press (1967) 352 p.

<u>PSYCHOLOGY</u>

21. Edited by Davey, Graham C. L. <u>PHOBIAS: A Handbook of Theory, Research andTreatment</u> New York, Wiley (1997) 451 p.

22. Edited by Hollin, Clive R. <u>CONTEMPORARY PSYCHOLOGY: AN INTRODUCTION</u> Bristol, PA. Taylor & Francis (1995) 216 p.

23. Goldberg, Jane G. (Jane Gretzner) <u>THE DARK SIDE OF LOVE: The Positive Role of Our Negative Feelings</u> New York, G. P. Putnam's Sons (1993) 306 p.

PSYCHIC ABILITY

24. Rhine, J. B. <u>EXTRA-SENSORY PERCEPTION</u> Boston, B. Humphries (1964), 240 p.

25. Connel, R. (Pseudonymn) <u>HEALING THE MIND: How Extra-Sensory Perception Can Be Used In The Investigation and Treatment of Psychological Disorders</u> London, Aquarian Press (1997) 190 p.

26. Cavanna, Roberto <u>ESP EXPERIMENTS WITH LSD 25 AND PSILOCYBIN: A METHODICAL APPROACH</u> New York, Parapsychology Foundation (1964) 123 p.

27. Todesch, Kevin J. <u>EDGAR CAYCE ON THE AKASHIK RECORDS: THE BOOK OF LIFE</u> Virginia Beach, VA, A. R. E. Press (1998) 181 p.

28. Editors of Time-Life Books <u>SECRETS OF THE INNER MIND</u> Alexandria, VA, Time-Life Books (1993) 144 p.

PHILOSOPHY/RELIGION

29. Watts, Alan <u>ZEN</u> Stanford, CA (1948) 41 p.

30. Danielom, Alain <u>YOGA: MASTERING THE SECRETS OF MATTER AND THE UNIVERSE</u> Rochester, VT, Inner Traditions (1991) 195 p.

31. <u>THE BUDDHA AND HIS TEACHINGS</u> Berkeley, CA, Dharma Publishing (1995) 381 p.

32. Keith, Arthur Berriedale <u>THE RELIGION AND PHILOSOPHY OF THE VEDA AND THE UPANISHADS</u> Westport, CT, Greenwood Press (1971) 683 p.

MISCELLANEOUS

33. Tolkien, J. R. R. <u>THE HOBBIT</u> New York, A Del Rey Book. (2001), 100 p.

34.   Bunker, M. N. <u>HANDWRITING ANALYSIS: THE SCIENCE OF DETERMINING PERSONALITY BY GRAPHOANALYSIS</u> Chicago, Nelson-Hall (1979), 256 p.

35.   Heindel, Max and Heindel, Augusta Foss <u>THE MESSAGE OF THE STARS</u> London, The Rosicrucian Fellowship (1973) 733 p.

<u>INDEX</u>

Extrasensory perception

F

Fantasy
    -controversial
    -harmful
    -productive
    -sexual
Flu
Force field
Freedom, compromise of
Freedom of expression
    -of choice

G

God
Guilt

H

Habits
Hallucination
Happy/unhappy distinction
Heaven
Herbivore
Heterosexuality
Holistic medicine
Homosexuality
Hugo, Victor
Hunches
Hygiene

I

Illness
Introspection

J

Jehova

Junk foods

K

Karma

L

Love/Hate
LSD

M

McFee, William
Masters, Sylvia, M. D.
Masturbation
Measles
Medical science
Meditation
    -body postures
    -rhythmic breathing
    -yogic method of
Mind/Brain
Morality
Multiple manifestations
Murder

N

Nakedness
Natural right
Netherworld
Nudism
Nudity

O

Omnivore
Orgasm
    -as spiritual experience
    -ecstasy of

ABOUT THE AUTHOR

F. Kipp Noyes has been a freelance writer for most of his adult life and has been regularly successful in having his work published. He has long been interested in philosophy, religion and parapsychology, among other intellectual pursuits. By combining these resources, he has written, *The Conquest of Misery*, an innovative discussion of the causes of and cures to the distress that plagues so many.

In writing this book and founding The Church of Psychic Sanctuary as a vehicle for implementing the ideas presented here, Mr. Noyes has offered a viable plan for ending misery on the planet. Through helping themselves by curing their own personal misery, many will begin to spread the word and contentment will reign.

www.ingramcontent.com/pod-product-compliance
Lightning Source LLC
Chambersburg PA
CBHW031316060726
47590CB00003B/1230